Klaus Wagener   Radko Ivanov Chapov

Floral Living

Dauerhafte Dekorationen ▪ Everlasting decorations

Sponsored by

Klaus Wagener, Radko I. Chapov

Vorwort & Foreword

Dauerhafte Frische

Dauerhafte Haltbarkeit und frische Wirkung müssen zueinander nicht im Widerspruch stehen. In unserem neuen Buch möchten wir dies beweisen und interpretieren das Thema Dauerfloristik neu. Drei konzeptionelle Ansätze waren uns dabei besonders wichtig.

Mit Orientierung an der Praxis haben wir unterschiedliche Räume und Raumsituationen gestalterisch erfasst, dabei auch den Outdoorbereich nicht ausgelassen. So wollen wir die Möglichkeiten dauerhaften Materials in Situationen, die mit Frischblumen und -pflanzen nicht realisierbar sind, hervorheben und dabei zeigen, wie ein überzeugender Frischeeffekt entsteht.

In der Realisation unserer Ideen haben wir das Augenmerk auf technisch sinnvolle und innovative Vorgehensweisen gelegt. Sie sind in vielen Step-by-Step-Erläuterungen und Tipps dokumentiert.

All unsere kreativen Einfälle sind in stilistische und farbgestalterische Themen eingeflossen. So wird dauerhafter Floralschmuck in jeweils passender Anmutung für vielfältige Wohnumgebungen, Businessräume oder gastronomische Locations vorstellbar.

Wir hoffen, Sie mit diesem Buch von den Möglichkeiten und Vorteilen dauerfloristischen Gestaltens zu überzeugen und Ihnen viele neue Anregungen zu geben. Wir meinen: Dauerfloristik ist ein großer Zugewinn für floristisches Gestalten, wenn sie Frische ausstrahlt, ohne den Aspekt der baldigen Vergänglichkeit zu beinhalten.

Viel Freude mit unseren Ideen und diesem Buch wünschen Ihnen

Everlasting freshness

Everlasting durability and freshness needn't stand in contradiction. Which is what we want to demonstrate in our new book, by reinterpreting the theme of permanent floral arrangements. Three conceptional approaches were particularly important to us.

With a focus on practical use, we designed arrangements for different room situations, also including outdoor areas. Our intention was to emphasize the possibilities created by permanent materials in situations where fresh flowers and plants cannot be implemented, and show how convincingly fresh they can look.

When implementing our ideas, we paid special attention to technically realistic and innovative approaches. We have documented these in numerous step-by-step descriptions and tips.

All our creative ideas are put together in style and colour themes. This makes it easier to imagine lasting floral decorations in individual designs for a variety of living environments, business rooms and gastronomy.

We hope this book will convince you of the many possibilities and advantages of permanent floral creations and also give you some new ideas. In our opinion, permanent florals represent an enormous gain for floristry designs, as they radiate freshness without the aspect of imminent transience.

Wishing you much joy with the ideas in our book,

Inhalt & Contents

Vorwort/ 002
Foreword

Impressum/ 144
Imprint

Dank/ 144
Thanks

■ Colourful & Charming 006 – 021
■ Sweet & Lovely 022 – 033
■ Blue & Fading 034 – 047
■ Classy & Romantic 048 – 059
■ Cosy & Delightful 060 – 075
■ Elegant & Precious 076 – 091
■ Exotic & Sprouting 092 – 109
■ Mellow & Rustic 110 – 123
■ Cool & Pure 124 – 141

004/005

Colourful & Charming

Frühlingserwachen

So zart Frühlingsblüten einerseits wirken, so kraftvoll versprühen sie andererseits ihre Farbenpracht, sobald der Winter zu Ende geht. Diese Farbenpracht und die Frische des Frühlings dauerhaft einzufangen, gelingt mit den vielfältigen farbgetreuen Nachbildungen von Tulpe, Narzisse & Co.

Spring awakening

While spring flowers appear delicate on the one hand, the power of their bright colours radiates as soon as winter comes to an end. These colours and the freshness of spring can be permanently captured with an array of artificial tulips, daffodils & Co. in colours that are as true as if they were real.

Bunte Stoffe und Papiere unterstützen das Frühlingsthema ebenso wie Gefäße und Accessoires aus Birke.

The spring theme is underlined with colourful fabrics and paper as well as containers and accessories made of birch.

Tips & Steps

008 / 009

(1) An einem dicken Birkenstamm oben einige Birkenäste mithilfe von Schrauben fixieren. (2) Daran mit unterschiedlichen Bändern und Kordeln die Floralien knoten. (3) Zum Schluss Birkenrindenkränzchen mit Bändern verzieren und auf die Astenden stecken.

(1) Screw several birch branches to a thick birch trunk. (2) Tie the florals to them with a selection of ribbons and string. (3) Finally, adorn small birch bark wreaths with ribbons and slip them over the tips of the branches.

…nstliche Frühlingsblumen, teils mit Zwiebeln (Gasper), Birkenzweige (Freese), Birkenrindenkränzchen, …irkenstamm mit Betonfuß (Freese), Bänder und Kordeln (Goldina), Schrauben, weitere im Bild sichtbare …emente: Tisch (Serax), Stühle (home24), Teppiche (Bloomingville)

artificial spring flowers, some with bulbs (Gasper), birch branches (Freese), small birch bark wreaths, birch trunk on a concrete foot (Freese), ribbons and strings (Goldina), screws, other elements visible in the picture: table (Serax), chairs (home24), rugs (Bloomingville)

Hasenfiguren bestimmen den Osteranlass für dieses Gesteck. Ohne sie versprüht der Floralschmuck auch nach Ostern noch lange seinen Charme.

Rabbits add Easter flair to this arrangement. Even without them the floral decoration continues to radiate its charm after the Easter celebrations are over.

künstliche Sommerblüten (Gasper), Birkenaststücke (Freese), trockene Gräser, Hasenfiguren (Gasper), Birkenschale (Gasper), Trockenblumensteckschaum-Ziegel (Oasis)

artificial summer florals (Gasper), chunks of birch branch (Freese), dried grasses, rabbits (Gasper), birch bowl (Gasper), dry floral foam bricks (Oasis)

Absolut angesagt und themenstimmig: Birkenrinde passt besonders gut zu frühlingshaftem Floralschmuck.

Absolutely trendy and in tune with the theme: Birch bark goes particularly well with spring floral decorations.

Nach dem Winter färben erste Frühblüher die Welt wieder bunt. Ihre kunstvollen Nachbildungen in Kiste und Korb stehen dem kaum nach.

As soon as winter has passed the first early bloomers add colour to the scenery. Artistic replicas in boxes and baskets are just as bright.

oben: künstliche Floralien (Gasper), Flechtenzweig, Birkenrindenkorb (Freese), Bänder (Goldina), Trockenblumensteckschaum-Ziegel (Oasis)

above: artificial florals (Gasper), lichened twig, birch bark basket (Freese), ribbons (Goldina), dry floral foam bricks (Oasis)

unten: künstliche Frühlingsblüten (Gasper), Zweigstücke, Birkenrinde (Freese), Birkenkästen (Gasper), Bänder (Goldina), Farbe, Trockenblumensteckschaum-Ziegel (Oasis)

below: artificial spring flowers (Gasper), twigs, bark (Freese), birch boxes (Gasper), ribbons (Goldina), paint, dry floral foam bricks (Oasis)

Diese kleinen Frühlings-
botengestecke eignen sich
als Mitbringsel ebenso,
wie als frei kombinierbare
Tischschmuckelemente.

These little arrangements
are harbingers of spring and
just as suitable for small gifts
or elements to be freely combined as table decorations.

012
———
013

nstliche Ranunkeln und weitere Floralien (Gasper), Rebengirlande und Birkenrindengefäße (beides eese), Steckdraht (Buco), Nähgarn, Trockenblumensteckschaum-Ziegel (Oasis), weitere im Bild sichtbare mente: Tisch (Serax), Stuhl (Home24)

artificial buttercups and other florals (Gasper), vine garlands and birch bark containers (both Freese), fixing wire (Buco), sewing thread, dry floral foam bricks (Oasis), other elements visible in the picture: table (Serax), chair (Home24)

Tips & Steps

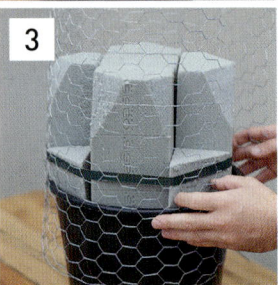

(1) Einen Kunststoffeimer als Basisgefäß für gute Standfestigkeit mit Steinen beschweren. (2) Trockenblumensteckschaum-Ziegel einfüllen. (3) Eimer und Steckschaum mit Drahtgeflecht umhüllen. (4) Diese Basisform in einen Leinensack setzen. (5) Den Sack mit Zeitungspapier ausstopfen und das Drahtgeflecht in Zwiebelform biegen. (6) Ton mit Kleister vermischen und Rupfenstücke damit tränken. (7) Die Zwiebelform mit den Rupfenstücken bedecken und diese vor dem Einstecken der Floralien gut durchtrocknen lassen.

(1) Weigh down a plastic bucket with rocks to make a stable base. (2) Fill with dry floral foam bricks. (3) Wrap the bucket and floral foam in chicken wire. (4) Place this base in a linen bag. (5) Stuff the bag with newspapers and bend the wire in the shape of a bulb. (6) Mix the clay and glue and soak pieces of burlap in it. (7) Cover the bulb shape with the burlap and allow to dry completely before inserting the florals.

künstliche Fritillarien und weitere Floralien (Gasper), Korkenzieherweide, Buchsbaumwurzelstöcke, Kaffeesack, Ton, Steckdraht (Buco), Drahtgeflecht, Tapetenkleister, Kunststoffeimer, Zeitungspapier, Trockenblumensteckschaum-Ziegel (Oasis), weitere im Bild sichtbare Elemente: Regal und Teppich (Bloomingville), Korb (D&M Depot), Vasen (Dutz und Serax)

artificial fritillaries and other florals (Gasper), corkscrew willow, box tree rootstocks, coffee bag, clay, fixing wire (Buco), chicken wire, wallpaper paste, plastic bucket, newspaper, dry floral foam bricks (Oasis), other elements visible in the picture: shelf and rug (Bloomingville), basket (D&M Depot), vases (Dutz and Serax)

Die Mehrzahl der Frühlingsblüher sind Zwiebelpflanzen. Da liegt es nahe, die Zwiebelform nachzubilden und mit Frühlingsblumenfülle zu krönen.

The majority of spring flowers are bulbous plants, so it makes sense to replicate the bulbous shape and top it off with an abundance of spring flowers.

links: künstliche Frühlingsblüher und Orchideenwurzeln (Gasper), Heu, Haften (Buco), Tapetenkleister, Tontöpfe, Zeitungspapier, Nähgarn

left: artificial spring flowers and orchid roots (Gasper), hay, pins (Buco), wallpaper paste, clay pots, newspaper, sewing thread

rechts: künstliche Frühlingsblüher (Gasper), Buchsbaumwurzelstöcke, Haften (Buco), Tapetenkleister, Packpapier, Tontöpfe, Zeitungspapier

right: artificial spring flowers (Gasper), box tree rootstocks, pins (Buco), wallpaper paste, packing paper, clay pots, newspaper

künstliche Floralien (Gasper), Rebengirlande und Metallgerüst mit Standplatte (Freese), Kaffeesack, Ton, Tapetenkleister, Wickeldraht und Steckdraht (Buco), Trockenblumensteckschaum-Kugel (Oasis)

artificial florals (Gasper), vine garland and metal frame on a stand (Freese), coffee sack, clay, wallpaper paste, binding wire and fixing wire (Buco), dry floral foam sphere (Oasis)

Tips & Steps

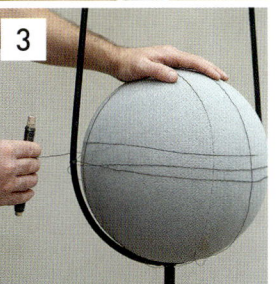

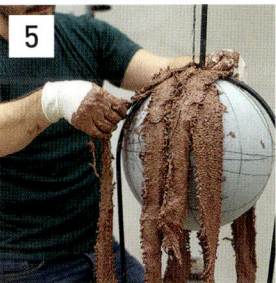
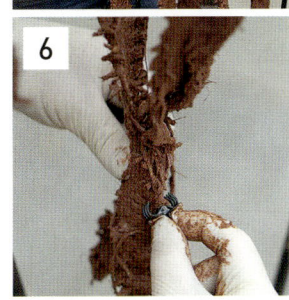

(1) Sackleinen oder Rupfen in Streifen schneiden. (2) Die Streifen in ein Gemisch aus Kleister und Ton tauchen. (3) Passende Trockenblumensteckschaum-Kugel mithilfe von Wickeldraht im Metallrahmen fixieren. (4) Das so vorbereitete Grundgerüst kopfüber aufhängen. (5) So können die noch feuchten Streifen hängend angebracht werden, bis die Kugel vollständig verdeckt ist. (6) Dann die Streifen unten zu zweit oder dritt zusammenfassen und durchtrocknen lassen. Grundform herumdrehen, in den Metallfuß setzen und mit den Textilfloralien bestecken.

(1) Cut coarse linen or burlap into strips. (2) Dip the strips into a mixture of glue and clay. (3) Fit a dry floral foam sphere into the metal frame and secure with binding wire. (4) Hang this base upside down. (5) Now the damp strips can be applied hanging down, until the entire sphere is covered. (6) Then the strips can be bound at the end in groups of two or three and allow to dry completely. Flip the construction upright again, place in the metal stand and adorn with textile florals.

Der Texturkontrast zwischen grobem Rupfen und den seidigen Blüten macht den besonderen Charme dieser Raumschmuckelemente in Tropfenform aus.

The contrast in textures between the rough burlap and silk flowers creates the charm of these teardrop-shaped room decorations.

Tips & Steps

(1) Trockenes Gras mit Wasser besprühen, um es flexibel zu machen. (2) Grasbüschel formen und mit Haften so auf einem Strohrömer befestigen, dass die Spitzen seitlich herabhängen. (3) Den mittig noch freien Streifen des Strohrömers mit Blüten behaften.

(1) Spray dried grass with water to make it flexible. (2) Bunch the grass together and attach the tufts to a straw wreath with pins, allowing the tips to hang over the sides. (3) Adorn the free strip on the top of the straw ring with flowers.

Mix aus künstlichen Frühjahrs- und Sommerforalien (Gasper), trockene Gräser, Haften (Buco), Strohrömer

mix of artificial spring and summer florals (Gasper), dried grasses, pins (Buco), straw wreath

Die Farbenfolge in diesen Frühlingskränzen entspricht weitgehend dem natürlichen Farbenkreis und erinnert an den Regenbogen bei einem sonnendurchfluteten Frühlingsregen.

The colour sequence in these spring wreaths is almost the same as the natural colour spectrum and is reminiscent of a rainbow during a sunlit spring shower.

018 / 019

x aus künstlichen Frühjahrs- und Sommerfloralien (Gasper), Flower Tape und Heißkleber (Oasis), Wellenahtring (Buco), weitere im Bild sichtbare Elemente: Birkenastbündel (Freese)

mix of artificial spring and summer florals (Gasper), flower tape and hot glue (Oasis), corrugated wire ring (Buco), other elements visible in the picture: bundles of birch branches (Freese)

Blühende Kirschzweige und Ranunkeln, deren Blühzeiten sich in freier Natur nur kurzfristig überlappen, sind in diesem Frühlingswandkranz dauerhaft miteinander verflochten.

Blossoming cherry twigs and buttercups, which bloom in nature briefly at the same time, are permanently intertwined in this spring wall wreath.

Tips & Steps

(1) Künstliche Kirschblütenzweige zum Kranz formen und mit Rebenbindedraht fixieren.
(2) Die weiteren Blüten ebenfalls mit Rebenbindedraht anbringen.

(1) Shape artificial cherry blossom twigs into a wreath and fasten with florist's twine. (2) Attach additional florals with florist's twine as well.

künstliche Ranunkeln und Kirschblütenzweige (Gasper), Rebenbindedraht (Buco)

artificial buttercups and cherry blossom twigs (Gasper), florist's twine (Buco)

Kränze aus Birkenrindenstreifen ergänzen den großen Wandkranz als formal passende Accessoires. In großer Ausführung können sie Gefäßfunktion für eine Frühlingsblütenkuppel erfüllen.

Wreaths made of birch bark strips are matching accessories selected for the large wall wreath. Make them a bit bigger and they can be used to hold a dome-shaped arrangement of spring flowers.

ben: künstliche Floralien (Gasper), Bänder (Goldina), Rebengirlande und Birkenrindenkränzchen (Freese), Haften und Steckdraht (Buco), Strohrömer

above: artificial florals (Gasper), ribbons (Goldina), vine garland and small birch bark wreaths (Freese), pins and fixing wire (Buco), straw wreath

unten: künstliche Ranunkeln (Gasper), Ranken, Zweige, Birkenrindenkranz (Freese), Bänder (Goldina), Trockenblumensteckschaum-Ziegel (Oasis), weitere im Bild sichtbare Elemente: Tisch (Serax)

below: artificial buttercups (Gasper), vines, twigs, birch bark wreath (Freese), ribbons (Goldina), dry floral foam bricks (Oasis), other elements visible in the picture: table (Serax)

Sweet & Lovely

Opulente Leichtigkeit

Die Opulenz üppig gewölbter Kugel- und Kuppelformen verbindet sich in diesem Thema mit der Zartheit und Leichtigkeit von Blüten in allen Nuancen von Rosa. Die schwerelose Wirkung wird durch Präsentationsweisen verstärkt, die die Kreationen fast schwebend erscheinen lassen.

Opulent lightness

The opulence of luxuriantly rounded spheres and dome shapes is combined in this theme with the delicacy and lightness of florals in all shades of pink. The weightless effect is enhanced with a presentation that makes the creations appear almost as if they were floating.

Diese Gestaltungsideen verzaubern Feste, bei denen vom Tischset bis zu Getränken und Nachtisch alles auf die Leichtigkeit und Süße der Farbe Rosa abgestimmt ist.

These design ideas enchant festivities where everything from the placemats to the drinks and desserts is colour-coordinated with the lightness and sweetness of pink.

Eine Gesteckform, die mit natürlichen Werkstoffen kaum zu realisieren ist, erhält durch die realitätsnahe Verschiedenartigkeit der textilen Päonienblüten eine besonders natürliche Wirkung.

An arrangement style that can hardly be created with natural materials is given a particularly natural look by the realistic diversity of fabric peonies.

künstliche Floralien (Gasper), Kätzchenzweige, Moos, Haften (Buco), Metallfuß, Heißkleber (Oasis), Trockenblumensteckschaum-Kugel (Oasis)

artificial florals (Gasper), pussy willow twigs, moss, pins (Buco), metal foot, hot glue (Oasis), dry floral foam sphere (Oasis)

Tips & Steps

(1) Trockenblumensteckschaum-Kugel halbieren und mit Moos behaften. (2) Den Kuppelbereich der Halbkugel mit Kätzchenweidenzweigen bestecken. (3) Den flachen Teil der Halbkugel mit Päonien-Blüten ausstecken. (4) Dabei auf eine ausgewogene Farbverteilung achten und eine harmonische Kuppelform ausbilden.

(1) Cut a dry floral foam sphere in half and base it with moss. (2) Insert willow twigs in the round side. (3) Insert peonies to cover the flat side of the foam. (4) Make sure to distribute the colours evenly while creating a harmonious dome shape.

künstliche Floralien (Gasper), geweißte Äste, Vasen (Gasper), Band (Goldina), Quarzsand, Steckdraht (Buco), Trockenblumensteckschaum-Kugel (Oasis)

artificial florals (Gasper), whitened branches, vases (Gasper), ribbon (Goldina), quartz sand, fixing wire (Buco), dry floral foam sphere (Oasis)

Kugelgestaltungen mit künstlichen, dauerhaften Werkstoffen haben gegenüber frischen Blütenkreationen wesentliche Vorteile. Hier entfällt vor allem die Wasserversorgung mit der daraus resultierenden Schwere einer mit Wasser vollgesaugten Steckschaumkugel sowie der Problematik des möglichen Austropfens.

Spherical arrangements with artificial, lasting materials have a considerable advantage over creations made of fresh florals. Most importantly, no water supply is needed, which also eliminates the added weight of a soaked floral foam sphere and the problem of potential water dripping.

Tips & Steps

(1) Textile Blüten, Trockenblumensteckschaum-Kugeln, Zierdraht, Wandfarbe in Rosa und Weiß, Holzstäbe und *Euphorbia spinosa* bereitlegen. (2) Steckschaumkugeln in Rosa und Weiß streichen. (3) Zierdraht in die Kranzöffnung einarbeiten, Kugeln zwischenklemmen und mit Holzstäben fixieren. (4) Blütenstiele in die Kugeln einstecken. Dann die Kranzgestaltung mit weißen Zweigruten durchstecken und damit in die Vase stellen.

(1) Lay out textile flowers, dry floral foam spheres, deco wire, pink and white paint, Tonkin sticks and *Euphorbia spinosa*. (2) Paint the floral foam spheres pink and white. (3) Work the deco wire into the centre of the wreath, fit the spheres in between and hold them in place with wooden sticks. (4) Insert flower stems in the spheres. Then slide the wreath arrangement onto the whitewashed rods and place in a vase.

künstliche Mohnblüten und Kirschblütenzweige (Gasper), trockene Euphorbientriebe, Zweigruten, Vasen (Gasper), Rankenkranz (Freese), Band (Goldina), Zierdraht (Buco), Quarzsand, Wandfarbe, Holzstäbe, Trockenblumensteckschaum-Kugeln (Oasis)

artificial poppies and cherry blossom twigs (Gasper), dried *Euphorbia* shoots, rods, vases (Gasper), vine wreath (Freese), ribbon (Goldina), deco wire (Buco), quartz sand, wall paint, wooden sticks, dry floral foam spheres (Oasis)

Die hier gezeigten Vasengestaltungen zeigen, welch weitreichende Möglichkeiten sich ergeben, wenn man auf Wasserversorgung keine Rücksicht nehmen muss.

The vase arrangements shown here demonstrate the many possibilities that open up when no water supply is required.

028 / 029

Tips & Steps

(1) Zunächst die grundlegende Kreisform des Gerüsts biegen und mit Wickeldraht fixieren. (2) Dann die Kuppelform aus Draht bilden und zugleich den Straußgriff formen. (3) Künstliche Ranken mit dünnen Bändern befestigen. (4) Schließlich die textilen Blüten einarbeiten und den Strauß so komplettieren.

(1) First bend wire into a circle for the frame and affix with binding wire. (2) Then shape the wire dome and the bouquet holder. (3) Attach artificial vines with thin ribbons. (4) Finally, work in the textile flowers to complete the bouquet.

nstliche Floralien (Gasper), Tillandsientriebe, Wurzeln, Vase (Gasper), Band (Goldina), Stoffstreifen, mantelter Spanndraht, Wickeldraht (Buco)

artificial florals (Gasper), *Tillandsia* shoots, roots, vase (Gasper), ribbon (Goldina), strips of fabric, tension wire, binding wire (Buco)

künstliche Floralien (Gasper), Birkenzweige, Weidenzweige, Band (Goldina), Wolle (Freese), Drahtgitter und Rebenbindedraht (Buco), Sprühfarbe, Trockenblumensteckschaum-Kugel (Oasis), weitere im Bild sichtbare Elemente: Stühle (Bloomingville), Kissen (Gasper)

artificial florals (Gasper), birch twigs, willow twigs, ribbon (Goldina), wool (Freese), wire mesh and florist's twine (Buco), spray paint, dry floral foam sphere (Oasis), other elements visible in the picture: chairs (Bloomingville), pillows (Gasper)

Da die Blütenkugeln nicht aus frischem Werkstoff gefertigt sind, können sie ohne Schaden zu nehmen gelagert und in immer wieder neuen Konstellationen eingesetzt werden, hier als Tischschmuck mit zusätzlicher Raumschmuckfunktion.

Since these floral balls are not made of fresh materials, they can be stored in good condition and reused several times in new compositions, for example these table decorations that double as room adornments.

künstliche Magnolie (Gasper), Lebensbaumzweige, Drilldraht (Buco), weitere im Bild sichtbare Elemente: Stühle (Serax und Bloomingville), Kissen (Gasper)

artificial Magnolia (Gasper), *Thuja* twigs, twist wire (Buco), other elements visible in the picture: chairs (Serax and Bloomingville), pillows (Gasper)

Mit dauerhaften Floralien ist es kein Problem, größere Räume angemessen und an gut sichtbarer Stelle, hier an der Decke aufgehängt, mit einem floralen Schmuck in passender Dimension zu versehen.

Permanent florals make it easier to properly decorate large rooms with floral arrangements in suitable sizes. They are also clearly visible when hung from the ceiling.

Tips & Steps

(1) Kahle Lebensbaumzweige mithilfe eines Drillgeräts und mit Drilldrähten aneinander fixieren. (2) So nach und nach eine große Kugelform bilden. (3) Zum Schluss in gleicher Weise die künstlichen Magnolienzweige hinzufügen.

(1) Attach bare *Thuja* twigs together with a hand drill and twist wire. (2) Keep adding twigs to gradually create a large ball. (3) Finally, add the artificial magnolias in the same fashion.

Blue & Fading

Maritime Symphonie

Die Farbe Blau wird, besonders in der warmen Zeit des Jahres, als erfrischend kühl wahrgenommen, erinnert sie doch an ein Bad in den Wellen und den weiten Himmel über dem Meer. Für Events im Freien und die Bar, in der man abends die blaue Stunde genießt, sind Gestaltungen in maritimem Blau die ideale Abrundung.

Maritime Symphony

Especially during the warmer time of year, the colour blue is perceived as refreshingly cool and it reminds us of a swim in the waves with endless sky stretching over the sea. For outdoor events and the bar where the blue hour can be enjoyed in the evening, floral arrangements in maritime blue provide the ideal finishing touch.

Glas, maritime Accessoires und wasserblaue Blüten sind unverzichtbar für Werkstücke mit diesem Thema.

Glass, maritime accessories and caerulean blue flowers are essential for workpieces in this theme.

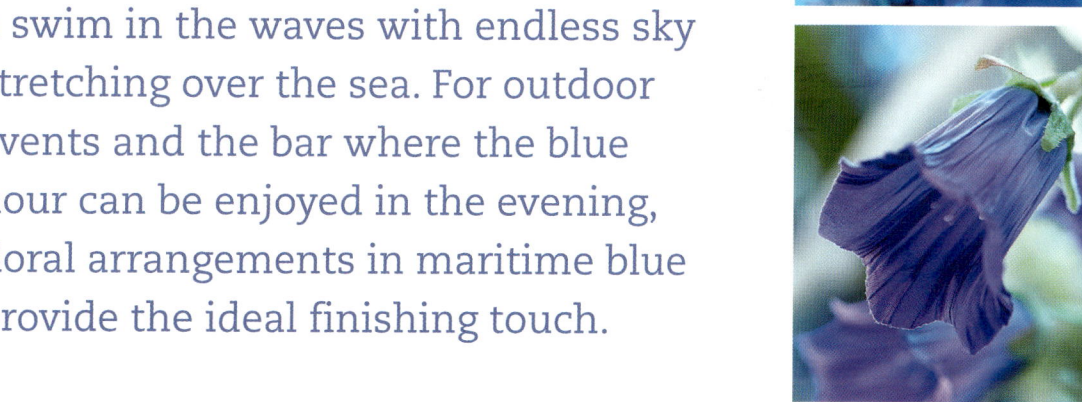

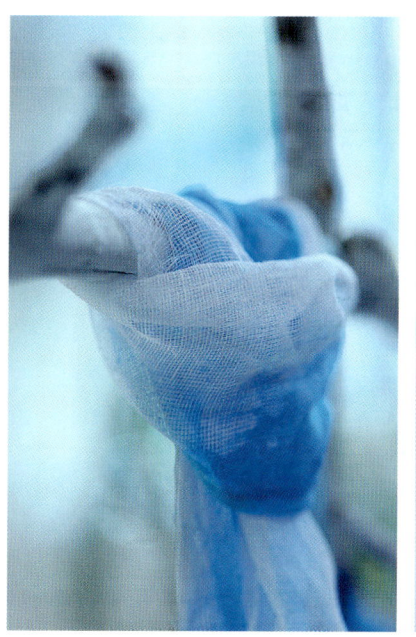

Die blaue Bar, ob als Strandpavillon oder in der City als Location für die After-Work-Party, gewinnt durch diesen Raumschmuck die passende floral-maritime Ausgestaltung. Dabei ist das Farbkonzept konsequent durchgeführt und die Form der Werkstücke ist von aufgestellten Surfbrettern abgeleitet.

The blue bar, whether as beach shack or a cool meeting place for an after-work party in the city, achieves the matching floral maritime look thanks to this room decoration. The colour scheme is consistently implemented and the shape of the workpieces is inspired by surfboards propped up against the wall.

Tips & Steps

036 / 037

(1) Zur Gestaltung der aus geweißten Zweigen gefertigten Grundgerüste mit Blütenketten werden zunächst Blüten je einer Art von ihren Stielen gezupft. (2) Rebenbindedraht dient als Trägermaterial, auf dem die Blüten nach dem Aufwickeln mithilfe von Myrtendraht nicht verrutschen können.

(1) To create the basic frames of whitewashed twigs and flower chains, the flower heads are first plucked from their stems. (2) Florist's twine provides support for the flower chains, which are wrapped and held in place with myrtle wire.

nstliche Sommerblüten (Gasper), Seesternskelette, Band und Kordel (Goldina), Seile (Freese), Ständer t Betonfuß (Freese), blaue Folie, Myrtendraht (Buco), Heißkleber (Oasis)

artificial summer flowers (Gasper), dried starfish, ribbon and string (Goldina), ropes (Freese), stand with concrete foot (Freese), blue foil, myrtle wire (Buco), hot glue (Oasis)

Tips & Steps

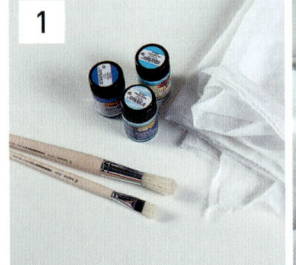

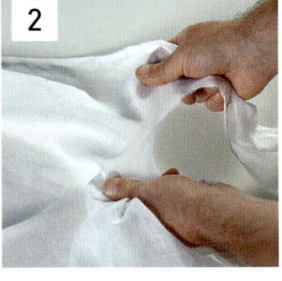

Fast körperlos-wässrig und damit nahezu schwerelos erscheint dieser Stoffkranz, der von Sommerblüten bekrönt wird.

This fabric wreath crowned with summer flowers appears disembodied and almost watery and therefore nearly weightless.

(1) Textilfarbe in unterschiedlichen Blautönen, durchschimmernden Stoff und Pinsel bereitlegen. (2) Stoff in ca. 10 cm breite Streifen reißen. (3) Die Stoffstreifen partiell mit einer der Textilfarben einpinseln. (4) Das Changieren zwischen den Blautönen und dem Weiß des Stoffs erzielt den Effekt, dass der Stoff nahezu schwerelos und wie Wasser wirkt.

(1) Lay out textile dye of various shades of blue, transparent fabric and a paintbrush. (2) Tear the fabric in strips approx. 10 cm in width. (3) Brush on the dye in stripes of different colours. (4) The interchanging shades of blue on the white fabric make it appear weightless like flowing water.

künstliche Sommerblüten und Tillandsienranke (Gasper), Band und Kordel (Goldina), Stoff, Textilfarben, Strohrömer, Haften (Buco), Heißkleber (Oasis), Teller (D&M)

artificial summer flowers and Tillandsia vines (Gasper), ribbon and string (Goldina), fabric, textile dye, straw wreath, pins (Buco), hot glue (Oasis), plate (D&M)

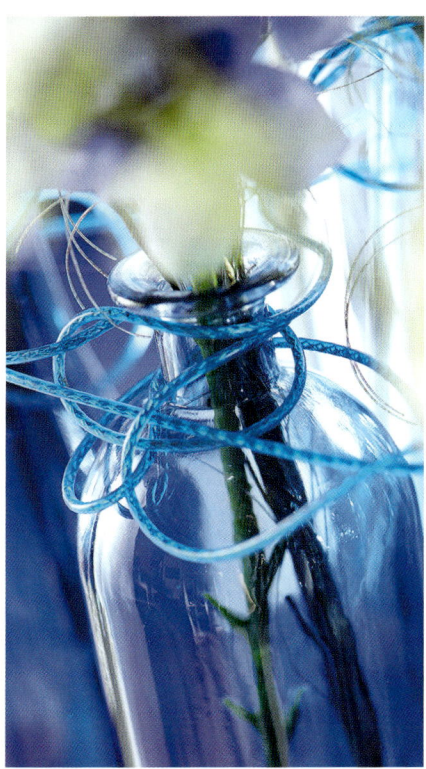

038 / 039

Die erfrischende Kühle von Wasser wird in dieser Gestaltung durch Flaschen aus blauem Glas vermittelt.

The refreshing coolness of water is relayed in this arrangement by blue glass bottles.

nstliche Floralien (Gasper), geweißte Zweige, Tabletttisch (Freese), Flaschen (teils Gasper), Wäsche- hnur, Band (Goldina), Stoff, Textilfarben, Trockenblumensteckschaum-Ziegel und Heißkleber (Oasis)

artificial florals (Gasper), whitened twigs, tray table (Freese), bottles (partly Gasper), clothesline, ribbon (Goldina), fabric, textile dye, dry floral foam bricks and hot glue (Oasis)

Maritime Dekorations-artikel vom ausgewaschenen Pflanzentrieb über Gehäuse von Meeresschnecken mit ihrem Perlmuttglanz bis zum Seestern stützen das frische Thema in Blau und Weiß.

The fresh theme in blue and white is supported by maritime deco articles, from rinsed plant shoots and sea snail shells with shiny mother-of-pearl to starfish.

Bild links unten: sommerliche Kunstfloralien (Gasper), Band (Goldina), Glasgefäß, Acryl-Eisstücke, Myrtendraht (Buco), Heißkleber (Oasis)

photo bottom left: artificial summery florals (Gasper), ribbon (Goldina), glass container, acrylic ice cubes, myrtle wire (Buco), hot glue (Oasis)

Bild rechts: sommerliche Kunstfloralien (Gasper), Peddigrohr, Meeresschneckenhäuser, Band (Goldina), Flaschen (Gasper), Wickeldraht, Myrtendraht (beides Buco), Floraltape (Oasis)

photo right: artificial summer florals (Gasper), can sea snail shells, ribbon (Goldina), bottles (Gasper), binding wire, myrtle wire (both Buco), floral tape (Oasis)

Bild rechts: künstliche Sommerfloralien und Tillandsien (Gasper), gebleichte Weidenstäbe, Meeresschneckenhäuser, Kunststoffnetz, Gefäß (Gasper), Trockenblumensteckschaum-Ziegel (Oasis)

photo right: artificial summer florals and Tillandsia (Gasper), bleached willow sticks, sea snail shells, plastic netting, container (Gasper), dry floral foam bricks (Oasis)

040/041

Bild links oben: künstliche Sommerfloralien (Gasper), gebleichte Wurzelstöcke, Zierdraht (Buco), Band Goldina, Trinkhalme

photo top left: artificial summer florals (Gasper), bleached roots, deco wire (Buco), ribbon (Goldina), drinking straws

Bild links unten: künstliche Sommerfloralien (Gasper), geweißte Rindenstücke Seesternskelette, Glasgefäß (Gasper), Kordel (Freese), Myrtendraht (Buco)

photo bottom left: artificial summer florals (Gasper), whitewashed pieces of bark, dried starfish, glass container (Gasper), string (Freese), myrtle wire (Buco)

> Solche floralen Vorhanggestaltungen sind ein imposanter Schmuck und dienen zugleich der Strukturierung eines großen Garten- oder Terrassenbereichs.
>
> Such floral curtain creations are an impressive decoration and at the same time provide a partition for a large garden or terrace.

künstliche Hortensien und Rittersporn (Gasper), geweißte Äste, Ständer mit Betonfuß (Freese), Wolle (Freese), Band (Goldina), Baumwollstoff, Textilfarbe, Kabelbinder, Wickeldraht (Buco), Heißkleber (Oasis), weitere im Bild sichtbare Elemente: Hocker (Broste), Kissen (teils Gasper, teils Broste)

artificial hydrangea and larkspur (Gasper), whitewashed branches, stand with concrete foot (Freese), wool (Freese), ribbon (Goldina), cotton fabric, textile dye, cable ties, binding wire (Buco), hot glue (Oasis), other elements visible in the picture: stool (Broste), pillows (Gasper and Broste)

Tips & Steps

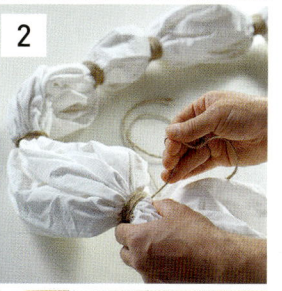

1 (1) Zum Färben des Stoffs in Batik-Technik Baumwollstoff, Farbe, Färbesalz und Kordel sowie Handschuhe zum Schutz der Hände bereitlegen. (2) Den Stoff raffen und in gewissen Abständen mit Kordel zusammenbinden. (3) Färbebäder in unterschiedlicher Farbintensität vorbereiten und den Stoff teils in das eine, teils in das andere Bad eintauchen. (4) Die Kordelumwicklungen bewirken die Farbverläufe. (5) Die Textilblüten schließlich mit Heißkleber auf dem Stoff fixieren.

(1) To dye the fabric with a batik effect, lay out cotton fabric, dye, dyeing salt and string, as well as gloves to protect your hands. (2) Gather the fabric and tie together with string at regular intervals. (3) Prepare dye baths in various colour intensities and dip the fabric partly in one and partly in the other. (4) The string wrappings create the colour gradient. (5) Hot-glue textile flowers to the fabric.

042 / 043

Tips & Steps

(1) Leinwand, Wandfarbe, Pinsel, Kabelbinder zum Aufhängen des Stoffs und Kordel zum Aufnähen der Floralien bereitlegen. (2) Die Leinwand in eine dreieckige Segelform schneiden, mit der Wandfarbe einstreichen und trocknen lassen. (3) Die Floralien mithilfe einer großen Stopfnadel und starker Kordel auf den Stoff nähen. (4) Kreuzstiche wirken hierbei besonders dekorativ. Ösen und Kabelbinder dienen schließlich zum Aufhängen des floralen Segels.

(1) Lay out canvas, wall paint, paintbrush, cable ties to hang the fabric and string for sewing on the florals. (2) Cut the canvas into a triangular sail shape, brush on the paint and allow to dry. (3) Sew the florals to the fabric with a large darning needle and strong string. (4) Cross stitches are particularly decorative here. Eyelets and cable ties are used to hang the finished floral sail.

künstliche Sommerfloralien (Gasper), geweißte Äste, Band (Goldina), Betonfuß, Leinwand, Kabelbinder, Nietösen, Kordel, Wandfarbe

artificial summer florals (Gasper), whitened branches, ribbon (Goldina), concrete foot, canvas, cable ties, eyelets, string, wall paint

Die Form eines kopfüber aufgehängten Segels, das vorherrschende Blau und die ausgebleichten Zweige verbreiten maritimes Flair auf der Terrasse.

The shape of an inverted sail, the dominant colour blue and the bleached branches all spread maritime flair on the terrace.

Der Korb aus sonnengebleichtem Schwemmholz wirkt maritim. Verstärkt wird diese Anmutung durch das Blau der Blüten, das durch die Wollkordel variiert wird.

The basket made of sun-bleached driftwood has a maritime look, which is enhanced by the blue flowers and tone-in-tone wool string.

künstliche Sommerfloralien (Gasper), Moos, Korb und Wolle (Freese), Haften (Buco), Trockenblumensteckschaum-Ziegel (Oasis)

artificial summer florals (Gasper), moss, basket and wool (Freese), pins (Buco), dry floral foam brick (Oasis)

046 / 047

Die mit Klammern fixierte Rolle aus gefärbten Leinwandstreifen und blauer Maulbeerbaumrindenfaser gibt den Kunstfloralien ihren Halt.

Artificial florals are given support by strips of dyed canvas and blue mulberry bark fibres rolled together and fastened with clothespins.

…nstliche Sommerfloralien (Gasper), gebleichte Wurzelstöcke, Schale (Depot), Leinwand, Wäscheklam-
…rn, Maulbeerbaumrindenfaser, Trockenblumensteckschaum-Ziegel (Oasis), Wandfarbe, weitere im Bild
…htbare Elemente: geprägte Blechquadrate (Affari)

artificial summer florals (Gasper), bleached roots, plate (Depot), canvas, clothespins, mulberry bark fibres, dry floral foam brick (Oasis), wall paint, other elements visible in the picture: embossed metal squares (Affari)

Classy & Romantic

Florale Romantik

Die romantische Ausstrahlung von Rosenblüten, eine dekorative Gestaltungsweise sowie opulent gewölbte Formen mit dichter Blütenfülle und zart überspielenden Ranken bestimmen die Kreationen in diesem Thema. Sie passen als florale Schmuckelemente in Räume und Außenbereiche, die von klassischer Architektur und entsprechendem Interieur geprägt werden.

Floral romance

The creations in this theme are determined by the romantic charm of roses, a decorative design concept and opulently domed shapes with densely packed flowers and delicately trailing vines around them. They look good as floral decorations for rooms and outdoor areas that are characterized by classic architecture with corresponding interiors.

In das klassisch-romantische Thema fügen sich geweißte Körbe und Holztabletts ebenso gut ein wie feines weißes Porzellan.

Whitewashed baskets and wooden trays go just as well with the classic and romantic theme as fine white porcelain.

Sträuße aus trockenen und textilen Floralien benötigen kein Wasser und können auf Metallständern mit stabilisierendem Betonfuß in wirkungsvoller Höhe positioniert werden, hier als doppelter Eingangsschmuck.

Bouquets of dried and textile florals don't need any water and can be positioned on metal stands with a stabilizing concrete foot at an impressive height, here as twin entrance decorations.

Tips & Steps

(1) Ein Kabelbinder am Metallstab dient als Stopper. (2) So kann der aufgesteckte Strauß am glatten Stab nicht herunterrutschen.

(1) A cable tie around the metal rod serves as a stopper. (2) This prevents the attached bouquet from sliding down the smooth rod.

künstliche Rosenblüten und Rosenzweige (Gasper), trockene Hortensienblütenstände, trockene *Craspedia*, trockenes Klettenlabkraut, trockene Wegraukentriebe, Band (Goldina), Metallständer mit Fuß (Freese), Kabelbinder

artificial roses and rose twigs, (Gasper), dried hydrangea inflorescence, dried *Craspedia*, dried cleavers, dried hedge mustard shoots, ribbon (Goldina), metal stand with foot (Freese), cable ties

Tips & Steps

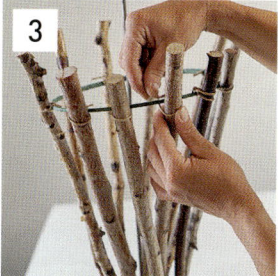

1 (1) Die Metallstange mit Betonfuß gibt Halt und Standfestigkeit für die Trichterform aus Ästen, Drahtring, Gummiringen und Rebenbindedraht. (2) Birkenäste mithilfe von Gummiringen am unteren Ende des Metallstabs bündelartig befestigen und die Bindestelle mit Wolle umwickeln. (3) Die Äste trichterförmig auseinanderspreizen und den mit Tape bewickelten Wellendrahtring oben mit Rebenbindedraht fixieren. (4) Heu in den Trichter einfüllen. (5) Trockenblumensteckschaum auf den Metallstab stecken. (6) Trockenranken und -triebe über den Steckschaum legen, Blüten einstecken und Zierdraht über die Blüten ziehen.

050 / 051

(1) A metal rod with a concrete foot provides support and stability for the funnel shape made of sticks, a wire ring, rubber bands and florist's twine. (2) Bundle the birch branches around the bottom of the metal rod and hold in place with rubber bands, then wrap wool around the tying point. (3) Spread the branches in a funnel shape and insert the corrugated wire ring wrapped in tape at the top; affix with florist's twine. (4) Fill the funnel with hay. (5) Skewer dry floral foam on the metal rod. (6) Arrange dry vines and shoots over the floral foam, insert florals and drape deco wire over the flowers.

stliche Rosenblüten und Rosenzweige (Gasper), Heu, trockenes Klettenlabkraut, Birkenäste und Wolle ese), Metallstange mit Betonfuß (Freese), Rebenbindedraht und Zierdraht (Buco), Wellendrahtring co), Gummiringe, Floral Tape und Trockenblumensteckschaum-Ziegel (Oasis)

artificial roses and rose twigs (Gasper), hay, dried cleavers, birch branches and wool (Freese), metal rod with concrete foot (Freese), florist's twine and deco wire (Buco), corrugated wire ring (Buco), rubber bands, floral tape and dry floral foam brick (Oasis)

Diese auf geweißten Holztabletts gefertigten Tischschmuckelemente können als Module lange Zeit immer wieder neu in beliebiger Zahl und Anordnung positioniert und kombiniert werden.

These table decorations on whitened wooden trays can be reused over time and positioned and combined in any number and constellation you like.

künstliche Rosenblüten und -zweige sowie Jasminranken (Gasper), trockene Ranken, Heu, Holzbrett (Freese), Holzstäbe, Haften (Buco), Trockenblumensteckschaum-Ziegel (Oasis), weitere im Bild sichtbare Elemente: Sets und Servietten (Chilewich), Gläser (Zwiesel)

artificial roses and twigs, jasmine vines (Gasper), dried vines, hay, wooden board (Freese), wood sticks, pi (Buco), dry floral foam bricks (Oasis), other elements visible in the picture: placemats and serviettes (Chilewich) glasses (Zwiesel)

052 / 053

Tips & Steps

1

(1) Trockenblumen-steckschaum-Ziegel mit mehreren Holzstäben verbinden. (2) Die Seitenbereiche mithilfe von Drahthaften mit Heu bedecken. Dann die künstlichen Rosenblüten einstecken und feine Trockenranken über das Gesteck ziehen.

2

(1) Attach dry floral foam bricks and secure with wooden sticks. (2) Pin hay around the sides to conceal. Then insert the artificial roses and drape delicate dried vines over the arrangement.

Kunstvoll nachgebildete Gartenrosen, begleitet von trockenen Gräsern, sind auf gefußtem Holztablett positioniert. Das erhöht die wertige Anmutung und begünstigt die Verwendung als Schmuck für ein Kuchenbüfett.

Artistic replicas of garden roses are adorned with dried grasses and displayed on a raised wooden cake plate. This adds value and makes it a suitable decoration for a cake buffet.

künstliche Rosenblüten und -zweige sowie Jasminranken (Gasper), trockene Statice, trockenes Honiggras, Heu, Holzteller (Freese), Band (Goldina), Haften (Buco), Anchor Tape und Trockenblumensteckschaum-Ziegel (Oasis)

artificial roses, rose twigs and jasmine vines (Gasper), dried statice, dried soft-grass, hay, wooden plate (Freese), ribbon (Goldina), pins (Buco), anchor tape and dry floral foam bricks (Oasis)

Trocken-werkstoffe sind eine gute Ergänzung zu den textilen Floralien und unterstützen wesentlich eine natürliche Wirkung der Werkstücke.

Dried materials are great partners for textile florals and help make the workpieces appear natural.

Tips & Steps

054 / 055

(1) Zwei Steckschaum-Ziegel zusammenlegen und mithilfe eines Tellers in Zylinderform schneiden. (2) Dann die beiden Stücke mit Anchor Tape miteinander verbinden und den Zylindermantel mit Heu behaften. (3) Den unteren Zylinderrand mit einer Schere begradigen. Textile Rosenblüten sowie Gräser einstecken und den Seitenbereich mit Band und Kordel gestalten.

(1) Place two floral foam bricks side by side and cut into a cylinder shape with the help of a bowl. (2) Then join the foam with anchor tape and pin hay around the sides. (3) Level off the bottom edge with scissors. Insert textile roses and grasses and wrap decorative ribbon and string around the outside.

oben: künstliche Rosenblüten und -zweige sowie Sternblütenzweig (Gasper), trockene Statice, trockenes Klettenlabkraut, Heu, Moos, Glasschale, Zierdraht (Buco), Trockenblumensteckschaum-Ziegel (Oasis)

above: artificial roses and twigs, starflower twig (Gasper), dried statice, dried cleavers, hay, moss, glass bowl, deco wire (Buco), dry floral foam brick (Oasis)

Ob die romantischen, kompakten Rosengestecke in Glasschalen, geweißten Körben oder in Wollfilz und feinem Gerank gestaltet werden, ist wesentlich vom Stil der gedeckten Tafel abhängig, auf der sie ihren Charme entfalten sollen.

The style of the dining table will determine whether these romantic compact rose arrangements should be presented in glass bowls, whitened baskets or felt pots with delicate vine collars – but they all unleash their charm.

unten: künstliche Rosenblüten und Dilldolden (Gasper), trockene *Craspedia*, trockenes Klettenlabkraut, trockener Sauerampfer, trockene Hortensienblüten, Heu, geweißter Korb und Wollkordel (Freese), Trockenblumensteckschaum-Ziegel (Oasis)

below: artificial roses and dill umbels (Gasper), dried *Craspedia*, dried cleavers, dried sorrel, dried hydrangea, hay, whitened basket and wool cord (Freese), dry floral foam bricks (Oasis)

Tips & Steps

(1) Trockenblumensteck-schaum-Ziegel halbieren, mit Filzband umwickeln und dieses mit Haften fixieren. (2) Drahtgeflecht um den Würfel biegen und ebenfalls mit Haften fixieren. (3) Einen Kranz aus trockenen Ranken winden und um den oberen Rand der Steckbasis legen, die von oben mit Moos abgedeckt wird. Dann die künstlichen Rosenblüten einstecken und einige Ranken sowie Zierdraht über die Blüten ziehen.

(1) Cut a dry floral foam brick in half, wrap felt around it and pin. (2) Bend wire mesh around the cube and also affix with pins. (3) Wind a wreath of dried vines and place around the upper edge of the foam base, the top of which will be covered with moss. Then insert the artificial roses and drape a few vines and deco wire over the flowers.

nstliche Rosen (Gasper), trockenes Klettenlabkraut, Moos, Holztafeln (Freese), Wolle und Filzband eese), Haften (Buco), Drahtgeflecht und Zierdraht (Buco), Trockenblumensteckschaum-Ziegel (Oasis)

artificial roses (Gasper), dried cleavers, moss, wooden plates (Freese), wool and felt (Freese), pins (Buco), wire mesh and deco wire (Buco), dry floral foam brick (Oasis)

Trockenfloralien und Korbgefäße bedingen einen edlen Landhaus-Charakter, der in vielfältigen Raumsituationen natürlich-ursprünglich wirkende Akzente setzen kann, hier in einem neoklassizistischen Umfeld.

Dried florals and baskets have sophisticated cottage flair, which can add natural and earthy highlights to all kinds of rooms, such as the neoclassical setting here.

Tips & Steps

1

2

(1) Den Drahtkorb mit Heu füllen, aus trockenem Klettenlabkraut einen Kranz winden und auf den Korbrand legen. (2) Zwei Trockenblumensteckschaum-Ziegel mit Anchor Tape verbinden, in den Korb stellen und darum herum weiteres Heu in den Korb stopfen. Dann die künstlichen Floralien einstecken. Gräser hinzufügen und knicken.

(1) Fill the wire basket with hay and wind a wreath of cleavers and place on the rim of the basket. (2) Stick two dry floral foam bricks together with anchor tape, place in the basket and stuff more hay around them. Then insert the artificial florals. Add the grasses and kink in the middle.

künstliche Rosen und Fuchsschwanztriebe (Gasper), trockenes Klettenlabkraut, trockenes Honiggras, Heu, Drahtkorb (Gasper), Anchor Tape und Trockenblumensteckschaum-Ziegel (Oasis)

artificial roses and foxtail (Gasper), dried cleavers, dried soft-grass, hay, wire basket (Gasper), anchor tap and dry floral foam bricks (Oasis)

en: künstliche Rosen und Mimosen (Gasper), trockene Sternskabiosen, trockenes Klettenlabkraut, Moos, rb (Freese), Trockenblumensteckschaum-Ziegel (Oasis), weitere im Bild sichtbar Elemente: Tischsets hilewich), Gläser (Zwiesel)

above: artificial roses and mimosas (Gasper), dried starflower pincushions, dried cleavers, moss, basket (Freese), dry floral foam brick (Oasis), other elements visible in the picture: placemats (Chilewich), glasses (Zwiesel)

058 / 059

Tips & Steps

(1) Steckschaum in die Öffnung des Zweigkranzes einfügen. (2) Von der Seite an wenigstens drei Stellen Holzstäbe einstecken, um die Steckbasis zu fixieren. Die Basis vor dem Bestecken mit Heu abdecken.

(1) Place floral foam in the centre of the twig wreath. (2) Insert at least three wooden sticks through the sides to hold the foam base in place. Before inserting the florals, cover the basis with hay.

en: künstliche Rosen und weitere Floralien (Gasper), trockenes Klettenlabkraut, Heu, geweißter Zweig- nz und Holztablett mit Fuß (Freese), Holzstäbe, Trockenblumensteckschaum-Ziegel (Oasis)

below: artificial roses and other florals (Gasper), dried cleavers, hay, whitened twig wreath and wooden tray with foot (Freese), wooden sticks, dry floral foam brick (Oasis)

Cosy & Delightful

Mediterraner Genuss

Rosmarin, Basilikum und Thymian, dazu ein paar rote Pfefferbeeren, dieser Anblick weckt sofort Gedanken an mediterrane Genüsse. Das auf die private Küche ebenso wie auf die Gastronomie ausgerichtete Thema macht sich ganz bewusst die Tatsache zunutze, dass auch das Auge bei einem Festmahl genießt.

Mediterranean pleasures

Rosemary, basil and thyme, coupled with a few red pepper berries, immediately conjures up an image that makes you think of Mediterranean delights. This theme is made for both home and commercial kitchens with creations that are a feast for the eyes.

Kochutensilien aller Art, Gewürze, Öl- und Essigflaschen sowie entsprechende Dekorationsartikel unterstützen das Thema Küche und Kochen.

A jumble of cooking utensils, spices, oil and vinegar bottles, together with matching decorative items, team up to support the kitchen and cooking theme.

060 / 061

Tips & Steps

[1] Eine Europalette in einen kleinen und einen großen Teil zersägen. [2] Beide Teile wie hier gezeigt aufstellen, dann zusammenschieben und mit Kordel verbinden. [3] Zwischen den beiden Teilen Trockenblumensteckschaum-Ziegel einfügen und Blütenstiele einstecken. [4] Den vorderen Bereich mit Kräutertöpfen gestalten, die zuvor mit Wolle und Kordel umwickelt wurden.

[1] Saw a euro pallet into two uneven pieces. [2] Prop up both parts as shown here, then push them together and secure with string. [3] Fill the space between them with dry floral foam bricks and insert flower stems. [4] Decorate the front section with herb pots wrapped in wool and string.

künstliche Kräuter und Kräuterblüten sowie weitere künstliche Floralien (Gasper), Textil-Rosmarin und Textil-Basilikum im Betontopf (Gasper), Wolle und Kordel (Freese), Europalette, Trockenblumensteckschaum-Ziegel (Oasis), weitere im Bild sichtbare Elemente: Geschirr (Serax)

artificial herbs, herb inflorescence and other artificial florals (Gasper), textile rosemary and basil in cement pot (Gasper), wool and string (Freese), euro pallet, dry floral foam bricks (Oasis), other elements visible in the picture: dishes (Serax)

062 / 063

Eine Grundgestaltung mit dem Ausdruck von Rustikalität und unkomplizierter Spontaneität, kombiniert mit künstlichen Floralien, die Bezug zum Kochen und Essen haben, erzeugen ein Bild mediterraner Genussfreude.

A basic design with rustic flair and uncomplicated spontaneity, combined with artificial florals relating to cooking and eating good food, paints a picture of Mediterranean treats.

In diesen dauerfloristischen Schmuckkreationen für Gastronomieräume scheint die Grenze zwischen Dekorativem und Essbarem zu verschwimmen. Es hat den Anschein, als seien die Produkte gerade frisch auf dem Markt einkauft.

In these permanent floral arrangements for the gastronomy trade, the line between decorations and edibles seems to blur. You would swear that these products were fresh from the market.

künstliche Floralien (Gasper), trockene Bananenblattstücke, Pflanzschubladen (Freese), Holzlöffel, Pappschilder, Kordel, Nietösen, Trockenblumensteckschaum-Ziegel (Oasis)

artificial florals (Gasper), dried banana leaves, planting drawers (Freese), wooden spoons, cardboard sign, string, eyelets, dry floral foam bricks (Oasis)

064 / 065

tliche Blüten und Kräuter (Gasper), trockene Gräser, Metallgefäße, und Kordel (Freese), Pflanzender aus Edelstahl (Gasper), verschiedene Papiere

artificial flowers and herbs (Gasper), dried grasses, metal containers and string (Freese), stainless steel plant signs (Gasper), various papers

In diesen floral-gastronomischen Büfettschmuck sind die Rezepte zu den angebotenen Speisen integriert.

The recipes for the dishes being served are integrated in this floral gastronomic buffet decoration.

künstliche Floralien (Gasper), Buchsbaumzweige, Olivenbaumzweige, Holzkiste und Kordel (Freese), Frühstücksbretter, verschiedene Papiere, Trockenblumensteckschaum-Ziegel (Oasis), weitere im Bild sichtbare Elemente: Drahtkorb (Gasper)

artificial florals (Gasper), box tree branches, olive branches, wooden box and string (Freese), breakfast plates, various paper, dry floral foam bricks (Oasis), other elements visible in the picture: wire basket (Gasper)

Während einige der Zutaten zu diesem Arrangement natürlich und haltbar sind, wurden die schnell welkenden Frischkräuter durch ihre künstlichen Nachbildungen ersetzt.

While some of the ingredients in this arrangement are natural and perishable, fresh herbs which wilt quickly have been replaced with their artificial cousins.

066 / 067

...stliche Olivenbaumzweige, künstlicher Lavendel, Basilikum und Rosmarin (alle Gasper), Buchsbaum...zeln, trockener Lavendel, Pfefferbeeren, Ingwerrhizome, Zwiebeln, Schale (Freese), Leinwand, Gewürz-...e, Holzschale, Kordel, Myrtendraht (Buco), weitere im Bild sichtbare Elemente: Drahtkorb (Gasper)

artificial olive branches, artificial lavender, basil and rosemary (all Gasper), box tree roots, dried lavender, pepper berries, ginger roots, onions, dish (Freese), canvas, herb plant, wooden bowl, string, myrtle wire (Buco), other elements visible in the picture: wire basket (Gasper)

Tips & Steps

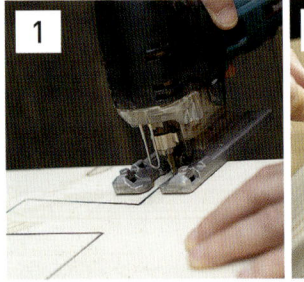

[1] Aus einem größeren Brett Frühstücksbretter mit Griff aussägen. [2] Graue Farbe mit Wasser vermischen und die Bretter damit lasieren. [3] Auf jedes Brett einen Textilkräutertopf legen, beides mit Trauerweidenruten umschlingen und diese mit Drilldraht fixieren.

[1] Saw a large board into breakfast plates with handles. [2] Mix grey paint with water and base the boards with it. [3] Lay a pot of textile herbs down on each board and wrap both with willow rods and secure with twist wires.

künstliches Basilikum im Topf (Gasper), Trauerweidenruten, Brett, Farbe, Drilldraht (Buco)

artificial basil in pots (Gasper), weeping willow rods, board, paint, twist wire (Buco)

068 / 069

künstliche Kräuter (Gasper), trockene Gräser, Steckdraht und Wickeldraht (Buco), Strohrömer, weitere im Bild sichtbare Elemente: Rankenkränze (Freese), künstlicher Olivenbaum (Gasper), grüne Flasche (Gasper), Holzkiste (Freese)

artificial herbs (Gasper), dried grasses, fixing wire and winding wire (Buco), straw wreath, other elements visible in the picture: vine wreaths (Freese), artificial olive tree (Gasper), green bottle (Gasper), wooden box (Freese)

künstlicher Lavendel und künstliche Wurzelranken (Gasper), trockene Zweige, Windlichtgläser (Gasper), Rebenbindedraht (Buco), Trockenblumensteckschaum-Ziegel (Oasis)

artificial lavender and artificial roots (Gasper), dried twigs, glass storm lanterns (Gasper), florist's twine (Buco), dry floral foam bricks (Oasis)

Für die gastronomische Verwendung ist die variable Kombinierbarkeit der Einzelelemente ebenso wichtig wie die Robustheit der verwendeten Werkstoffe. Beides weisen diese Gefäßgestaltungen auf.

Being able to combine individual elements in various ways is just as important for use in restaurants as the durability of the materials used. These container arrangements meet both criteria.

stliche Hortensienblüten und Himbeeren (Gasper), künstliche Lavendel- und Olivenbaumzweige sper), trockenes Chinaschilf, Flaschen (Gasper), Kordel, Myrtendraht (Buco)

artificial hydrangeas and raspberries (Gasper), artificial lavender and olive branches (Gasper), dried Chinese reeds, bottles (Gasper), string, myrtle wire (Buco)

In dieser Kollektion getrockneter Kräuterbündel setzen künstliche Lavendelähren belebende Farbakzente.

In this collection of bundled dried herbs, artificial lavender flowers add refreshing colour accents.

künstlicher Lavendel und künstliche Wurzelranken (Gasper), trockener Wollziest, trockene Färberdisteln, trockener Oregano, trockene *Craspedia*, trockene *Calendula*, trockene Eukalyptuszweige, Wolle und Metallring (Freese), Kordel, Drilldraht (Buco)

artificial lavender and artificial roots (Gasper), dried lamb's ear, dried safflower, dried oregano, dried *Craspedia*, dried *Calendula*, dried *Eucalyptus* twigs, wool, metal ring (Freese), string, twist wire (Buco)

Textile Küchenschellenblüten und Edelweiß weisen dieses mit trockenen Chilischoten akzentuierte Gesteck-Duo als Schmuck für Restaurants mit alpinem Ambiente aus.

Textile pasque flowers and edelweiss define this duet arrangement for a restaurant decoration with alpine character, highlighted with dried chillies.

stliches Edelweiß (Gasper), künstliche Küchenschelle und Klettentriebe (Gasper), trockene Gräser, ckener Sauerampfer, trockene Chilischoten, Birkenreisigmatte (Freese), Steckdraht (Buco), Trocken- menstecksteckschaum-Ziegel (Oasis), weitere im Bild sichtbare Elemente: künstliche Feigenbäume (Gasper), schen und Tassen (Gasper)

artificial edelweiss (Gasper), artificial pasque flowers and Arctium shoots (Gasper), dried grasses, dried sorrel, dried chilli peppers, birch twig mat (Freese), fixing wire (Buco), dry floral foam bricks (Oasis), other elements visible in the picture: artificial fig trees (Gasper), bottles and cups (Gasper)

Tips & Steps

[1] Trockenblumensteckschaum-Ziegel in die Gitterkörbe stellen und rundherum mit trockenen Gräsern und Kräutern verdecken. [2] Dann die künstlichen Floralien in dichter Fülle einstecken.

[1] Place dry floral foam bricks in the wire baskets and cover with dried grasses and herbs. [2] Then insert the artificial florals in a dense arrangement.

künstliche Sommerfloralien (Gasper), trockene Gräser und Kräuter, Gitterkörbe (Gasper), Trockenblumensteckschaum-Ziegel (Oasis)

artificial summer florals (Gasper), dried grasses and herbs, wire baskets (Gasper), dry floral foam bricks (Oasis)

Mohn und Margeriten, Dahlien und Rispentomaten weisen diese Tisch- und Wandschmuckgestaltungen als florale Ergänzungen eines sommerlichen Festessens aus.

Poppies and daisies, dahlias and tomatoes on the vine all identify these table and wall decorations as floral elements fit for a summer feast.

074 / 075

Tips & Steps

[1] Hartriegelzweige mit Kordel an die Holzmatten knoten.
[2] Künstliche Blütenstiele mit Wolle umwickeln. Dann die künstlichen Floralien ebenfalls mit Kordel an den Matten fixieren.

[1] Tie dogwood twigs to the wooden laths with string.
[2] Wrap artificial flower stems with wool. Then tie the artificial florals to the laths with string as well.

stliche Dahlien und Tomatenrispen (Gasper), rotrindige Hartriegelzweige, trockene Gräser, trockene, leichte Okraschoten, Wolle (Freese), Driftholzmatte (Gasper), Gewürztaschen, Kordel, Heißkleber (Oasis)

artificial dahlias and vine tomatoes (Gasper), red dogwood twigs, dried grasses, dried and bleached okras, wool (Freese), driftwood laths (Gasper), spice bags, string, hot glue (Oasis)

Elegant & Precious

Vornehme Blütenpracht

Große Blüten in feinen Pastelltönen und mit exquisiten Formen haben eine edle Ausstrahlung und spielen in floralen Kreationen ihren dominierenden Charakter aus. Wo sie nicht alleine und mit nur wenigen Begleitelementen wirkungsvoll ihren Charme versprühen, stehen sie unter ihresgleichen in prachtvollem Prunk zusammen.

Elegant abundance of flowers

Showy flowers in delicate pastel shades with exquisite shapes have an elegant aura and play a dominating role in floral creations. As they effectively radiate their charm, not alone but coupled with only a few other elements, they put on a show of rich grandeur.

Schimmerndes Perlmutt und vielfältige Papiertexturen vom handgeschöpften Büttenpapier bis zum transluzenten Pergamin ergänzen die edlen Blütenschönheiten in diesem Thema perfekt.

Shimmering mother-of-pearl and a variety of paper textures, from handmade paper to translucent glassine, make a perfect match for the elegant flower beauties in this theme.

Tips & Steps

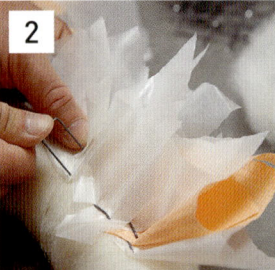

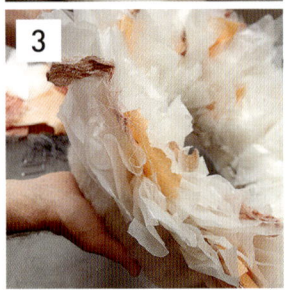

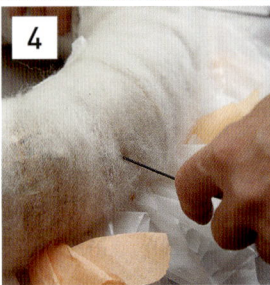

[1] Strohrömer mit Wolle bewickeln. [2] Stücke von verschiedenen Papieren gemischt auf den Kranz haften. [3] So die Oberseite des Kranzes dicht füllen. [4] Steckdrähte an drei bis vier Stellen in den Strohkranz stecken. [5] Damit den Woll-Papier-Kranz in der Öffnung des Flechtkranzes fixieren. [6] Orchideenrispen, Ranken und Blätter in den Flechtkranz integrieren.

[1] Wrap a straw wreath with cotton wool. [2] Pin assorted bits of paper onto the wreath. [3] Densely pack the top of the wreath with paper. [4] Insert three or four fixing wires along the sides of the straw ring. [5] These will hold the wool and paper wreath in place in the centre of the larger wreath. [6] Integrate orchid panicles, vines and leaves in the outer wreath.

Opulente und prunkende Wirkung einerseits, Leichtigkeit im Auftritt andererseits vereint dieser mit Orchideen besetzte Doppelkranz. Die Leichtigkeit in diesem Wandschmuck wird dabei durch die feinen Papiere, die durchbrochene Flechtweise des äußeren Kranzes und die hellen Farben bewirkt.

This double wreath adorned with orchids combines an opulent and impressive look with an air of lightness. The airiness of this wall decoration is created by the fine papers, the loose woven pattern in the outer wreath and the pale colours.

künstliche Orchideenrispen und Alokasienblätter (Gasper), trockene Waldrebenranken, trockene Grannenlilienblätter, Flechtkranz und Wolle (Freese), verschiedene Papiere, Strohrömer, Haften und Steckdraht (Buco), Heißkleber (Oasis), weitere im Bild sichtbare Elemente: Stühle (Fink), Kupferdrahtkörbe (Gasper), Glasvasen (Leonardo), Kordel-Schale (D&M Depot), Windlichter (Dutz)

artificial orchid panicles and Alocasia leaves (Gasper), dried *Clematis* vines, dried *Aristea* leaves, wicker wreath, wool (Freese), assorted papers, straw ring, pins, fixing wire (Buco), hot glue (Oasis), other elements visible in the picture: chairs (Fink), copper wire baskets (Gasper), glass vases (Leonardo), string bowl (D&M Depot), storm lanterns (Dutz)

078/079

oben: künstliche Orchideenblüten und weitere Floralien (Gasper), Flechtenzweige, trockene *Lunaria*, trockene Gräser, verschiedene Papiere, Holzschale (Freese), Zierdraht (Buco), Heißkleber (Oasis), weitere im Bild sichtbare Elemente: Windlichter (Gasper)

above: artificial orchids and other florals (Gasper), lichened twigs, dried *Lunaria*, dried grasses, assorted papers, wooden bowl (Freese), deco wire (Buco), hot glue (Oasis), other elements visible in the picture: storm lanterns (Gasper)

Hochwertige Papiere als Begleiter edler Blüten wirken nicht nur mit Farben und Texturen. Neue Struktureffekte lassen sich durch vielfältig variierende Schichtungen erzeugen, die den Blüten eine Bühne bieten.

High-quality paper accompanying elegant flowers not only has impact through its colours and textures. New structural effects can be created with diverse layering, which provides a stage for the flowers.

unten: künstliche Orchideenblüten und Alokasienblätter (Gasper), trockene Grannenlilienblätter, Flechtenzweige, verschiedene Papiere, Zweigobjekt (Freese), Heißkleber (Oasis)

below: artificial orchids and Alocasia leaves (Gasper), dried *Aristea* leaves, lichened twigs, assorted paper, twig item (Freese), hot glue (Oasis)

links: künstliche Orchideenrispen und Ranken (Gasper), trockene Gräser, Flechte, Holzschale (Freese), Heißkleber und Trockenblumensteckschaum-Ziegel (Oasis)

left: artificial orchids and vines (Gasper), dried grasses, lichen, wooden bowl (Freese), hot glue and dry floral foam bricks (Oasis)

080 / 081

rechts: künstliche Orchideenrispen und Ranken (Gasper), *Tillandsia xerographica*, Flechte, trockene *Lunaria*, verschiedene Papiere, Rankenkranz (Freese), Keramikfliese, Heißkleber und Trockenblumensteckschaum-Ziegel (Oasis)

right: artificial orchid panicles and vines (Gasper), *Tillandsia xerographica*, lichen, dried *Lunaria*, assorted papers, vine wreath (Freese), ceramic tile, hot glue and dry floral foam bricks (Oasis)

Tips & Steps

1 **2** **3** **4**

(1) Einen Zylinder aus Trockenblumensteckschaum schneiden und in den Rankenkranz einkleben. (2) Zweigbündel spiralförmig fassen und binden. (3) Das Bündel von unten in den Steckschaum einstecken. (4) Diese straußähnliche Form herumdrehen, die Straußkuppel mit Ranken umwickeln und diese mit Zierdraht fixieren. Dann von oben Blüten einstecken oder einkleben und Pergaminpapier in Streifen zwischen die Ranken flechten.

[1] Cut dry floral foam into a cylinder shape and glue into the vine wreath. [2] Tie a bunch of twigs in a spiral. [3] Insert the twig bundle in the bottom of the floral foam. [4] Upend this bouquet-like shape, wrap the vines around the dome and affix with deco wire. Then insert or hot-glue flowers all over the top and weave strips of glassine between the vines.

künstliche Floralien (Gasper), trockene Grannenlilienblätter, Zweige, Rankenkranz (Freese), Band (Goldina), Pergaminpapier, Zierdraht (Buco), Schale (Affari), Heißkleber und Trockenblumensteckschaum-Ziegel (Oasis)

artificial florals (Gasper), dried *Aristea* leaves, twigs, vine wreath (Freese), ribbon (Goldina), glassine, deco wire (Buco), dish (Affari), hot glue, dry floral foam brick (Oasis)

> So genannte Stehsträuße in flachen Schalen sind mit dauerhaften Werkstoffen problemlos zu realisieren, da eine Wasserversorgung entfällt.
>
> Standing bouquets in flat dishes are easy to make with permanent materials, as no water supply is required.

082 / 083

Bei allen stehend präsentierten Sträußen kommt es besonders auf den Stielbereich und eine perfekte Bindestelle an, da beide wesentliche Gestaltungselemente sind.

When bouquets are presented standing on their stems, special focus is on the stem area and a perfect tying point, since these are both significant design elements.

stliche Floralien (Gasper), trockene *Lunaria*, trockene Gräser und Wegraukentriebe, Flechtkordel dina), Pergaminpapier, Heißkleber (Oasis)

artificial florals (Gasper), dried *Lunaria*, dried grasses and hedge mustard shoots, woven string (Goldina), glassine, hot glue (Oasis)

Dieses florale Raumschmuckobjekt wirkt spannungsreich aufgrund des Formkontrasts zwischen der kompakten, geometrischen Kreisscheibe und den wuchshaft spielerischen Floralien.

This floral room decoration has an exciting dynamic due to the contrast between the compact, geometrical circular disc and the playful growth shapes of the florals.

künstliche Magnolien- und Holunderbeerenzweige (Gasper), trockene Gräser und *Lunaria*, Metallfuß (Freese), weißes Holzbrett, Raufasertapete, Abtönfarbe, Wollkordel, Steckdraht (Buco), Heißkleber (Oasis), Sprühfarbe und farbige Frischblumensteckschaum-Scheibe (Oasis), weitere im Bild sichtbare Elemente: Kerzenständer (Freese)

artificial magnolias and elderberry twigs (Gasper), dried grasses and *Lunaria*, metal foot (Freese), white wooden board, ingrain wallpaper, paint, wool string, fixing wire (Buco), hot glue (Oasis), spray paint and coloured floral foam disc (Oasis), other elements visible in the picture: candle holder (Freese)

Tips & Steps

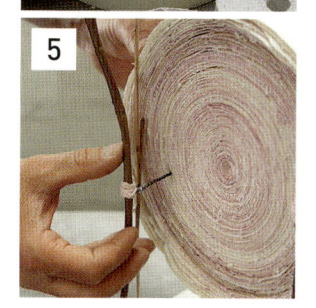

(1) Alle benötigten Floralien, Gestaltungsmaterialien, technischen Hilfsmittel und Werkzeuge bereitlegen. (2) Zunächst Raufasertapetenrolle mit einer Säge in Stücke schneiden. (3) Die entstandenen Rollen seitlich teilweise mit Farbe gestalten. (4) Nach dem Trocknen der Farbe die schmalen Rollen abrollen, mehrere Streifen aufeinanderlegen und erneut aufrollen. Die entstehende große Rolle auf die runde Steckschaumscheibe kleben und diese auch außen mit Tapete versehen. (5) Die Scheibe auf einen Metallfuß stecken. Floralien andrahten, die Drahtstelle mit Wollkordel kaschieren und die Stiele so an der Scheibe fixieren.

[1] Lay out all required florals, design materials, technical aids and tools. [2] First saw a roll of woodchip wallpaper into thin slices. [3] Daub strokes of paint on the sides. [4] After the paint has dried, unroll the slim rolls, stack several strips on each other and roll them together again. Glue this new large roll onto the floral foam disc and additionally cover the foam with wallpaper around the outside. [5] Insert a metal foot in one side of the disc. Wire the florals and conceal the wires with wool string, at the same time attaching the stems to the disc.

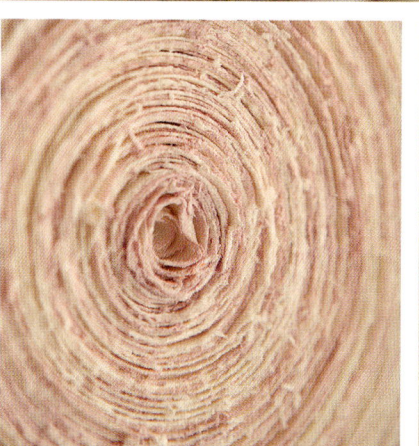

084/085

Diese Gruppe floral akzentuierter Säulen ist in der Anordnung frei variierbar und kann in verschiedenen Situationen und an unterschiedlichen Stellen in einem Raum Akzente setzen.

This group of pillars highlighted with florals can be freely arranged and positioned in different situations to add accents to a room.

künstliche Magnolie (Gasper), *Viburnum rhytidophyllum*, trockene Zweige, Zylindergläser (Gasper), Furnier (Greengate), Naturbast (Freese), Zierdraht (Buco), Tapete, Flechtkordel, Stecknadeln, Pinholder und Knetkleber (Oasis), Heißkleber und Trockenblumensteckschaum-Ziegel (Oasis)

artificial magnolias (Gasper), *Viburnum rhytidophyllum*, dried twigs, glass cylinders (Gasper), veneer (Greengate), natural bast (Freese), deco wire (Buco), wallpaper, woven cord, pins, pinholders and adhesive putty (Oasis), hot glue and dry floral foam bricks (Oasis)

Tips & Steps

086 / 087

(1) Steckschaum zylinderförmig zum Durchmesser der zu verwendenden Vasen passend zurechtschneiden. Aus unterschiedlichen Materialien Rollen bilden und auf die Steckschaumzylinder kleben. (2) Diese auch seitlich mit dem jeweiligen Material verkleiden. (3) Die Zylinderformen mit Pinholdern auf den Vasen befestigen. Magnolien- und Trockenzweige außen mit Band und Zierdraht an den floralen Säulen fixieren.

[1] Cut floral foam in cylindrical shapes to fit the vases. Fashion rolls of various materials and stick these on top of the foam cylinders. [2] Use the same material to adorn the sides as well. [3] Attach the cylinder shapes to the vases with pinholders. Affix the magnolias and dried twigs to the sides of the floral pillars with ribbon and deco wire.

Tips & Steps

[1] Kopierpapier in Quadrate schneiden, als Markierung diagonal falten. [2] Alle Ecken zur Mitte hin falten. [3] und [4] Das so gefaltete Papier wenden und den Faltvorgang mit den Ecken wiederholen. [5] Die Form erneut wenden und mit den Fingern in die zu öffnenden Ecken greifen. [6] Diese nun vorsichtig öffnen, so dass das Papierobjekt schließlich die hier gezeigte Form aufweist. [7] Einige solcher Papierobjekte herstellen und dicht an dicht mit Perlkopfnadeln auf dem Steckschaum befestigen. Hierbei für sicheren Halt jede Nadel eventuell mit einem Tropfen Heißkleber versehen. [8] Wenn die Papierobjekte die Steckschaumscheibe nahezu vollständig bedecken, die künstlichen Floralien aufkleben. Jetzt kann diese Gestaltung als Mittelteil in den hängenden Raumschmuck integriert werden.

[1] Cut printer paper into squares, fold diagonally to mark the centre. [2] Fold all the corners to the centre. [3] and [4] Flip the folded paper over and repeat the folding process with the corners. [5] Turn it over again and slip you fingers into the corners. [6] Carefully open the corners to give the paper the shape shown here. [7] Create several of these paper objects and attach them with beaded pins to the floral foam in a dense arrangement. For a secure hold you might add a drop of hot glue to each needle. [8] Once the folded papers almost completely cover the floral foam disc, glue on the artificial florals. This creation can now be integrated in the centre of the hanging room decoration.

künstliche Phalaenopsisblüten, Tillandsienranken und Platanenfrüchte (Gasper), trockene Grannenlilienblätter, gebleichte *Phormium*-Blätter, trockene *Lunaria*, geweißte Ast-Kreisscheiben (Freese), Furnierstreifen, Kordel (Lehner), Kopierpapier, Schnur, Heißkleber (Oasis), Perlkopfnadeln und farbige Frischblumensteckschaum-Scheibe (Oasis), weitere im Bild sichtbare Elemente: Stühle (Fink)

artificial Phalaenopsis orchids, Tillandsia vines and plane tree fruits (Gasper), dried *Aristea* leaves, bleac *Phormium* (leaves, dried *Lunaria*, whitened wood discs (Freese), veneer strips, cord (Lehner), printer pape string, hot glue (Oasis), beaded pins, coloured floral foam disc (Oasis), other elements visible in the pict. chairs (Fink)

Die Gleichheit der Grundform aller drei in unterschiedlicher Ausführung kreierter Elemente bedingt die gestalterische Geschlossenheit dieses hängenden Raumschmuckobjekts.

The similar basic shape of all three elements, each with its own design, creates the uniform look of this hanging room decoration.

088

089

Papiere und papierähnliche Produkte lassen sich nicht nur farblich perfekt mit Blüten kombinieren, auch die Texturen dieser Produkte ähneln den Oberflächenausprägungen pflanzlicher Werkstoffe und ihrer kunstvollen Nachbildungen.

Paper and paper-like products can not only be combined perfectly with flowers in terms of colour, their textures are also similar to the surface characteristics of both fresh and artificial floral materials.

künstliche Lilien und Zweige (Gasper), trockene *Lunaria*, trockene Gräser, Kordel-Schale (D&M Depot), verschiedene Papiere und papierähnliche Produkte, Schlagmetall, Tackerklammern, Sprühkleber und Trockenblumensteckschaum-Ziegel (Oasis)

artificial lilies and twigs (Gasper), dried *Lunaria*, dried grasses, rope bowl (D&M Depot), assorted papers paper-like products, metal leaf, staples, spray glue and dry floral foam bricks (Oasis)

Die Rollen scheinen als alternative Steckhilfen zu fungieren. Basis ist jedoch Steckschaum, der für frische Lilien nass sein müsste und die Papierverwendung verhindern würde. Hier zeigt sich ein Vorteil dauerhafter Floralien.

The rolls of paper appear to be holding the lilies as an alternative insertion base. If real flowers were used they would require soaked floral foam, which would not work well with the paper. Another obvious advantage of using permanent florals.

Exotic & Sprouting

Dschungel-Feeling

Exotische Herkunft, extravaganter Ausdruck der Form und eine Dominanz der Farbe Grün bedingen die belebende Wirkung der Kreationen in diesem Thema. Insbesondere Räume, die funktionsbedingt nüchtern gestaltet sind, z. B. Büros, Flure und Empfangshallen, erhalten mit solchen tropisch anmutenden Naturausschnitten belebende Akzente.

Jungle feeling

Exotic origins, extravagant expressions of shape and dominating shades of green determine the invigorating effect of the creations in this theme. Especially functional rooms with simple designs, such as offices, hallways and entrance halls, are given refreshing highlights by such tropical representatives of nature.

> Alles Grüne und Aspekte des Zufälligen, wie Craquelé und Verlaufsglasuren, unterstützen das exotisch-pflanzliche Thema.
>
> The exotic plant theme is enhanced by all things green and irregular details, such as craquelé and dripping glaze techniques.

Kreise und kreisende Bewegungen sind die Formprinzipien dieses Raumschmucks. Die Orchideenblüten und die weiteren Floralien in den Fruchtschalen auf dem Bretterkreis scheinen bestätigen zu wollen, dass die Natur in der Lage ist, jeden Raum zu besiedeln.

Circles and circular movement are the form principles of this room decoration. The orchids and other florals in fruit cups displayed on the circular board apparently want to demonstrate that nature can colonize any room.

094 / 095

...stliche Werkstoffe (Gasper), *Zea mays*, *Lecythis zabucajo*, *Bertholletia excelsa*, Maulbeerbaumrinde, ...del, runde Holzplatte, Myrtendraht (Buco), Schrauben, weitere im Bild sichtbare Elemente: Stuhl (Affari)

artificial materials (Gasper), *Zea mays*, *Lecythis zabucajo*, *Bertholletia excelsa*, mulberry bark, string, round wooden board, myrtle wire (Buco), screws, other elements visible in the picture: chair (Affari)

Die Anmutung eines hängenden Gartens geht von diesen auf Elementen aus dicken Bambusrohren basierenden Raumschmuckformen aus.

These room decorations based on thick elements made of bamboo tubes have the look of a hanging garden.

künstliche Werkstoffe (Gasper), Luffa, Bambus (Freese), Canna-Stäbe, Rebenbindedraht und Zierdraht (Buco), Myrtendraht und Drilldraht (Buco), Kordel (Goldina), Holzlatten, Farbe, Schrauben

artificial materials (Gasper), loofah, bamboo (Freese), canna sticks, florist's twine and deco wire (Buco), myrtle wire and twist wire (Buco), string (Goldina), wooden slats, paint, screws

096/097

Tips & Steps

(1) Den Rand einer Holzkreisscheibe mithilfe eines Tackers mit geknautschtem Pergamin gestalten. (2) Blätter falten bzw. rollen und auf die Platte tackern. (3) Zum Schluss künstliche Orchideenblüten andrahten und einstecken.

(1) Bunch glassine together and staple around the edge of a round wooden disc. (2) Fold or roll leaves and also staple them to the board. (3) Finally, wire artificial orchids and insert.

künstliche Blätter, Wurzeln und Orchideenblüten (Gasper), Holzkreisscheibe, Pergamin, Steckdraht (Buco), Tackerklammern, weitere im Bild sichtbare Elemente: Buddhafigur (Gasper), Holzbox (Bloomingville), Schale (Broste)

artificial leaves, roots and orchids (Gasper), wooden disc, glassine, fixing wire (Buco), staples, other elem visible in the picture: Buddha figure (Gasper), wooden box (Bloomingville), bowl (Broste)

Tips & Steps

1 **2**

(1) Trockenblumensteckschaum-Kegel mit Wandfarbe streichen.
(2) Textile Grasblätter um den Kegel wickeln und mit Stecknadeln fixieren. Dann am Kegelfuß die übrigen Floralien einstecken und den Kegel mit der Spitze nach unten weisend aufhängen.

(1) Brush wall paint onto dry floral foam cones. (2) Wrap textile grass leaves around the cone and fix in place with pins. Then insert the other florals in the foot of the cone and hang with the tip pointing down.

1 **2**

(1) Eine in Grün gestrichene Trockenblumensteckschaum-Kugel locker und teilweise mit schlanken textilen Gräsern überziehen. (2) Eine hohle Halbkugel aus Styropor dicht mit kreuz und quer geführten, breiten Gräsern gestalten und die Kugel hineinlegen. Dann die abfließenden Werkstoffe und Orchideenblüten hinzufügen.

(1) Wrap a few slim blades of textile grass loosely around a green-painted dry floral foam ball. (2) Densely wrap broad blades of grass around a hollow Styrofoam semi-sphere in a dense criss-cross pattern and place the ball inside. Then add the flowing materials and orchids.

098 / 099

tliche Blätter, Gräser, Ranken und Orchideenen (Gasper), Wandfarbe, Kordel, Steckdraht), Stecknadeln, Trockenblumensteckschaum- l (Oasis)

artificial leaves, grasses, vines and orchids (Gasper), wall paint, string, fixing wire (Buco), pins, dry floral foam cone (Oasis)

künstliche Gräser, Ranken und Orchideenblüten (Gasper), Wandfarbe, Stecknadeln, Heißkleber (Oasis), Styroporhalbkugel und Trockenblumensteckschaum-Kugel (Oasis)

artificial grasses, vines and orchids (Gasper), wall paint, pins, hot glue (Oasis), Styrofoam semi-sphere and dry floral foam ball (Oasis)

künstliche Grünwerkstoffe (Gasper), *Musa textilis*, *Cocos nucifera*, Kakteenskelett, Metallplatte mit Stäben, Wolle (beides Freese), Drilldraht (Buco)

artificial greens (Gasper), *Musa textilis*, *Cocos nucifera*, dried cactus, metal plate with rods, wool (both Freese), twist wire (Buco)

Diese Raumschmuckskulpturen sind pflanzliche Reminiszenzen an die Tropen und ihre Regenwälder. Der Kontrast zwischen den trockenen, braunen Werkstoffen und Frischgrünem intensiviert die Raumwirkung.

These room deco sculptures are floral reminiscences of tropical lands and their rain forests. The contrast between the dried, brown materials and the fresh greens intensifies the spatial effect.

Tips & Steps

(1) Trockenblumensteckschaum-Ziegel mithilfe von Korkrindenstücken in einem Drahtkorb festklemmen. (2) Zweige und künstliche Werkstoffe unter Einsatz eines Drillgeräts mit Drilldrähten fixieren.

(1) Wedge dry floral foam bricks in a wire basket using chunks of cork bark. (2) Affix twigs and artificial materials with a hand drill and twist wires.

stliche Tropenfloralien (Gasper), Korkrinde, Zweige, Metallkorb auf Fuß (Freese), Drilldraht (Buco), ckenblumensteckschaum-Ziegel (Oasis)

artificial tropical florals (Gasper), cork bark, twigs, metal basket on a foot (Freese), twist wire (Buco), dry floral foam bricks (Oasis)

Als Teil der Gestaltung kontrastieren die auf dieser Doppelseite gezeigten Gerüste aus Ästen und Zweigen mit ihrer konstruktiven Form das Wuchshafte der künstlichen Pflanzen.

As part of the design, the constructive look of the framework of branches and twigs on these two pages stands in contrast to the shapes of the artificial plants.

künstliche Tropenfloralien (Gasper), Moos, Aststücke, Birkenrindenquadrate und Wollkordel (Freese), Wickeldraht und Steckdraht (Buco), Schrauben, Trockenblumensteckschaum-Ziegel (Oasis)

artificial tropical florals (Gasper), moss, branch pieces, birch bark rectangles and wool string (Freese), winding wire and fixing wire (Buco), screws, dry floral foam bricks (Oasis)

Zusätzlich fungieren diese Gerüste als haltgebende Elemente und ersetzen eine Wandaufhängung. So können diese floralen Raumschmuckkreationen jederzeit versetzt werden, ohne Spuren zu hinterlassen.

These frames not only support the floral arrangements, but also eliminate the necessity to hang them on a wall. Therefore, these floral room decorations can be moved around flexibly without leaving a trace.

102 / 103

...stliche Tropenfloralien (Gasper), Aststücke, Zweige, bewurzelte Efeuranken, Zierdraht (Buco), Wickel-...ht und Drilldraht (Buco), Kabelbinder

artificial tropical florals (Gasper), branch pieces, twigs, ivy vines with roots, deco wire (Buco), winding wire and twist wire (Buco), cable ties

Die epiphytische Lebensweise tropischer Orchideen, Farne und mancher Sukkulenten ist Grundlage der Gestaltung dieses raumgreifenden Floralschmucks.

The design of this expansive floral decoration is based on the epiphytic growth habit of tropical orchids, ferns and certain succulents.

Tips & Steps

(1) Aus den Zweigen und Ästen mithilfe von Drilldraht ein Gerüst herstellen. (2) Den mittigen Stamm und die Holzgefäße mit Schrauben fixieren. Steckschaum einfüllen und Werkstoffe einstecken.

(1) Create a framework of branches and twigs and secure with twist wires. (2) Position the stem and the wooden containers in the centre and affix with screws. Fill with dry floral foam and insert the materials.

künstliche tropische Werkstoffe (Gasper), Äste und Zweige, Holzgefäße (Freese), Drilldraht (Buco), Schrauben, Trockenblumensteckschaum-Ziegel (Oasis)

artificial tropical florals (Gasper), branches and twigs, wooden containers (Freese), twist wire (Buco), scre dry floral foam bricks (Oasis)

104 / 105

Ein gebogenes Baustahlgitter dient als Grundform für ein dauerhaftes Werkstück, das in Flechttechnik und mithilfe von Drilldrähten gefertigt ist. Orchideen und Anthurien setzen darin blühende Akzente.

A construction of bent steel rebar provides the base for a permanent workpiece made with a weaving technique and twist wires. Orchids and anthuriums add blooming highlights.

künstliche Werkstoffe: Orchideen, Anthurie, Tillandsienranke, Alokasienblätter, Philodendronblatt, Gräser (alle Gasper), Äste und Zweige, Holzfurnier, Baustahlgitter, Drilldraht (Buco)

artificial materials: orchids, anthuriums, Tillandsia shoots, Alocasia leaves, Philodendron leaf, grasses (Gasper), branches and twigs, wood veneer, steel rebar, twist wire (Buco)

106/107

Tips & Steps

(1) Zweige und Ästen am gebogenen Baustahlgitter mit Drilldraht befestigen. (2) Künstliche Gräser und grasähnliche Werkstoffe in die Baustahlmatte einflechten. (3) Blatt- und Blütenstiele im Werkstück mittels Klemmtechnik fixieren.

(1) Attach branches and twigs to the bent rebar with twist wires. (2) Weave artificial grasses and grass-like materials through the grid. (3) Affix leaf and flower stems in the workpiece using a clamping technique.

> Weiße Gloriosenblüten beleben dieses dauerfloristische Flechtgitter und erinnern an eine Gruppe tropischer Schmetterlinge, die sich für eine kleine Pause darauf niedergelassen haben.
>
> White Gloriosa blossoms invigorate this everlasting woven mesh of florals and are reminiscent of a kaleidoscope of tropical butterflies that have set down to take a quick break.

künstliche Werkstoffe: Gloriosenblüten, Sansevierienblätter, Orchideenwurzeln und Tillandsienranken (alle Gasper), *Musa textilis*, Mikado-Stäbe, Lianenstücke, Holzfurnier, Seile, Betonfuß mit Metallstäben (Freese), Wickeldraht (Buco)

artificial materials: Gloriosa lilies, Sansevieria leaves, orchid roots and Tillandsia shoots (all Gasper), *Musa textilis*, Mikado sticks, liana, veneer, ropes, concrete foot with metal rods (Freese), winding wire (Buco)

Wie ein dreidimensionales, von beiden Seiten zu betrachtendes, freistehendes Bild ist dieser Raumschmuck im Metallrahmen konstruiert und gestaltet.

This room decoration in a metal frame is constructed and arranged in a way that makes it appear like a three-dimensional, free-standing picture that can be observed from both sides.

stliche Werkstoffe: Orchideen, Alocasien- und Anthurienblätter, Mooskraut, Ranken und Orchideenwurzeln (alle Gasper), Hopfenranken, geweißte *Ibicella lutea*, Rahmen mit Betonfuß (Freese), Wickeldraht (Buco)

artificial materials: orchids, Alocasia and Anthurium leaves, spike moss, vines and orchid roots (all Gasper), hops vines, whitened *Ibicella lutea*, frame with concrete foot (Freese), winding wire (Buco)

Mellow & Rustic

Landhaus-Sommer

Der überbordende Reichtum des Hoch- und Spätsommers, einer Zeit gleichzeitiger Blütenpracht und Fruchtreife, wird in einem ländlich-edel anmutenden Stil eingefangen. Natürlichkeit und handwerkliche Ursprünglichkeit in zeitgemäßer Interpretation fließen in den dauerhaft haltbaren Kreationen zusammen.

Cottage summer

The exuberant wealth of mid- and late-summer – a season of flowering splendour and ripe fruit – is captured in a rural, elegant style. Naturalness and handcrafting origins in a contemporary interpretation come together in permanent arrangements.

Neben sonnengesichtigen Blüten sind es rustikal-raue Texturen und Flechtstrukturen, die zu diesem ländlich anmutenden Thema gehören.

Alongside the sunny-faced flowers, rustic and rough textures combine with woven patterns to make up this country theme.

künstlicher Sommerflor (Gasper), trockene Hortensientriebe, Getreide, Stroh, Drahtgitter und Myrtendraht (Buco), Holzbretter, Schrauben, Tackerklammern, Trockenblumensteckschaum-Ziegel (Oasis)

artificial summer flowers (Gasper), dried Hydrangea shoots, wheat, straw, wire mesh and myrtle wire (Buco), wooden boards, screws, staples, dry floral foam bricks (Oasis)

Die Basis bzw. Umrandung dieses Gestecks ist abgeleitet vom bäuerlich-traditionellen Garbenbinden und Basteln mit Stroh. Die Blüten symbolisieren die spätsommerliche Fülle der Natur.

The fringed basis of this arrangement derives from rural-traditional grain binding and handcrafting with straw. The flowers symbolize the late summer abundance of nature.

Tips & Steps

(1) Spanplattenbretter zurechtsägen und zu einem Rechteckkasten zusammenschrauben. (2) Dabei bilden die kurzen Seiten des Kastens Standfüße und die Längsseiten bleiben schmaler. Das ermöglicht später im unteren Bereich des Gestecks Durchblicke, die der Gestaltung Leichtigkeit verleihen. Den Boden des Kastens mit Drahtgeflecht versehen. (3) Aus Stroh mit Myrtendraht dichte, spitz zulaufende Bündel wickeln. (4) Diese Bündel an den Kasten schrauben, wobei die Spitzen nach unten weisen und beim Hinstellen nach außen gebogen werden. (5) Steckschaum in den Kasten füllen, Blüten, Zweige und Getreidehalme einstecken.

(1) Saw chipboards into pieces and screw together to make a rectangular box. (2) The shorter sides of the box double as feet, while the narrower long sides are raised up off the table. Leaving a space to look through beneath the arrangement will add lightness to the creation. Line the bottom of the box with wire mesh. (3) Bunch straw into dense and tapered bundles and wrap with myrtle wire. (4) Screw these bundles to the box with the tips pointing downwards and curving outwards over the table. (5) Fill the box with dry floral foam and insert flowers, twigs and blades of wheat.

Tips & Steps

(1) Die künstlichen Gräser im großen Korb werden als Ganzes im Topf eingesetzt. **(2)** In den kleinen Korb Steckschaum einlegen, mit Moos abdecken und die künstlichen Blütenstiele einstecken.

(1) The artificial grasses in the large basket are inserted in pots. (2) Insert dry floral foam in a smaller basket, cover with moss and arrange the artificial flower stems.

künstliche Sonnenblumen, Rudbeckien, Begonienblätter und Gräser im Topf (alles Gasper), trockener Sauerampfer, Moos, Wurzelknorren (Freese), Körbe und Wollkordel (Freese), Steckdraht (Buco), Trockenblumensteckschaum-Ziegel (Oasis)

artificial summer flowers, Rudbeckia, Begonia leaves and grasses in pots (all Gasper), dried sorrel, mos gnarled roots (Freese), baskets and wool string (Freese), fixing wire (Buco), dry floral foam bricks (Oasis

Tips & Steps

114 / 115

1

(1) Weidenruten zu einem dicken Bündel zusammennehmen und mit Wickeldraht fixieren. (2) Den Flechtkranz über die Bindestelle schieben. (3) Blütenstiele und Schilf in das Bündel einstecken bzw. einklemmen.

2

(1) Gather willow rods in a thick bundle and wrap with winding wire. (2) Slide the wicker wreath over the tying point. (3) Insert flower stems and reeds into the bundle.

3

...tliche Sonnenblumen, Rudbeckien, Zierlauchblüten und Pfennigblatttriebe (alle Gasper), trockenes ...aschilf, Weidenruten, Flechtkranz (Freese), Wickeldraht (Buco)

artificial sunflowers, Rudbeckia, Allium flowers and moneywort shoots (all Gasper), dried Chinese silver grass, willow rods, wicker wreath (Freese), winding wire (Buco)

Tips & Steps

(1) Korkgranulatplatten in Stücke reißen und mit Heißkleber auf die Trockenblumensteckschaum-Kugeln kleben. (2) Trockene Gräser und *Lunaria* mit Stecknadeln fixieren. (3) Kugeln in die Töpfe legen und je eine künstliche Sonnenblumenblüte einstecken.

(1) Tear granulated cork sheets into pieces and hot-glue to the dry floral foam balls. (2) Affix dried grasses and *Lunaria* with pins. (3) Place the spheres in the pots and insert a single sunflower in each.

oben: künstliche Floralien (Gasper), Hafer, Gerste, trockene Gräser und Wurzeln, Wollkordel (Freese), Leinwand, Blechdosen, Myrtendraht (Buco), doppelseitiges Transparentklebeband und Heißkleber (Oasis)

above: artificial materials (Gasper), oat, barley, dried grasses and roots, wool cords (Freese), canvas, tin cans, myrtle wire (Buco), transparent double-sided tape and hot glue (Oasis)

unten: künstliche Sonnenblumen (Gasper), trockene Gräser und *Lunaria*, Korkgranulatplatten, Keramiktöpfe, Stecknadeln, Heißkleber und Trockenblumensteckschaum-Kugeln (Oasis)

below: artificial sunflowers (Gasper), dried grass and *Lunaria*, granulated cork sheets, ceramic pots, pins, hot glue and dry floral foam spheres (Oasis)

Tips & Steps

(1) Korb mit Stroh auslegen und einen mit Trockenblumensteckschaum gefüllten Kunststoffeimer mittig hineinstellen. **(2)** Blüten einstecken und von außen trockene Farnwedel mit Wollkordel anknoten.

(1) Line a basket with straw and place a plastic bucket filled with dry floral foam inside it. (2) Insert the flowers and arrange dried fern fronds around the outside and tie on with wool string.

oben: künstlicher Sommerflor (Gasper), trockene Euphorbientriebe, trockene Farnwedel, Stroh, Wollkordel (Freese), Korb, Kunststoffeimer, Trockenblumensteckschaum-Ziegel (Oasis)

above: artificial summer flowers (Gasper), dried *Euphorbia* shoots, dried fern fronds, wool string (Freese), basket, plastic bucket, dry floral foam bricks (Oasis)

unten: künstlicher Sommerflor (Gasper), *Lecythis zabucajo*, Getreide, trockene Gräser und Maisblätter, Brett (Freese), Haften (Buco), Schrauben, Trockenblumensteckschaum-Ziegel (Oasis)

below: artificial summer flowers (Gasper), *Lecythis zabucajo*, wheat, dried grasses and corn leaves, board (Freese), pins (Buco), screws, dry floral foam bricks (Oasis)

Strukturen und Texturen sind in diesen Gestaltungen nicht nur naturgegeben vorhanden, sondern entstehen durch Schichtungen, Faltungen und Verdichtungen vielfältig neu.

The structures and textures in these arrangements are not only naturally present, but are additionally created through numerous layering, folding and pressing techniques.

Tips & Steps

Flechtmatte in Streifen schneiden und diese zusammen mit trockenen Maisblättern hochkant wellenförmig in die quadratische Schale legen. Kleine Holzstücke dienen dabei als Abstandshalter.

Cut a woven straw mat into strips and arrange these together with dried corn leaves in perpendicular waves in the square dish. Small pieces of wood serve as spacers.

künstliche Sonnenblumen und weitere Floralien (alle Gasper), Kardendisteln, Maisblätter, trockene Gräser, Holzstücke, Flechtmatte, Schale, Trockenblumensteckschaum-Ziegel (Oasis)

artificial sunflowers and other florals (all Gasper), thistles, corn leaves, dried grasses, pieces of wood, woven straw mat, bowl, dry floral foam brick (Oasis)

Tips & Steps

Zwei Steckschaumziegel in Halbzylinderform schneiden, zusammenkleben und in die Schale legen. Korkrindenstücke anbohren, mit Holzstäben versehen und damit im Steckschaum fixieren. Oben künstliche Floralien einstecken.

Cut two dry floral foam bricks into cylinder halves, glue together and place in a dish. Drill holes in pieces of cork bark and insert wooden sticks, then affix around the dry floral foam. Insert artificial florals on the top.

Tips & Steps

Steckschaumkugel halbieren und eine Hälfte in die Schale legen. Baumpilze andrahten und seitlich einstecken. Dann künstliche Blüten einstecken, Gräser um die Blüten schlingen und mit Stecknadeln fixieren.

Cut a dry floral foam sphere in half and place in a dish. Wire tree mushrooms and fix around the sides. Then insert artificial flowers, add loops of grass around them and affix with pins.

oben: künstliche Sommerfloralien (Gasper), Clematisranken, Korkrinde, Stroh, Schale, Myrtendraht (Buco), Holzstäbe, Heißkleber und Trockenblumensteckschaum-Ziegel (Oasis)

above: artificial summer flowers (Gasper), *Clematis* vines, cork bark, straw, bowl, myrtle wire (Buco), wooden picks, hot glue and dry floral foam bricks (Oasis)

unten: künstliche Sommerfloralien (Gasper), trockene Gräser, Baumpilze (Freese), Schale, Steckdraht (Buco), Stecknadeln, Trockenblumensteckschaum-Kugel (Oasis)

below: artificial summer flowers (Gasper), dried grasses, tree mushrooms (Freese), bowl, fixing wire (Buco), pins, dry floral foam sphere (Oasis)

Tips & Steps

(1) Aus Steckschaum-Ziegeln einen großen Quader zusammenkleben. (2) Eine der oberen Ecken abschneiden. Korkgranulatplatten in Stücke reißen und diese aufkleben, ohne den Bereich der abgeschnittenen Ecke zu verdecken. Hier die Sonnenblumen sowie Getreide und Zweige einstecken.

(1) Stack dry floral foam bricks to create a rectangular cube and glue together. (2) Slice off one of the upper corners. Tear granulated cork sheets into pieces and glue onto the foam, without covering the cut-off corner. On this space insert the sunflowers, wheat and twigs.

künstliche Sonnenblumen und Rosen (Gasper), Birkenzweige, Weizen, Korkgranulatplatten, Heißkleber und Trockenblumensteckschaum-Ziegel (Oasis)

artificial sunflowers and roses (Gasper), birch twigs, wheat, granulated cork sheets, hot glue and dry flor foam bricks (Oasis)

Dieses Quader-Duett vereint konstruktiven Ausdruck mit Natürlichkeit und architektonisch wuchtige Präsenz mit dem Charme von Gewachsen-Organischem.

This cuboid duet combines constructive impact with naturalness and an architectural presence with the charm of organic materials.

künstliche Sommerfloralien (Gasper), Gerste, trockene Gräser, Baumstammstücke, Kaffeesack, Drahtgitter, Spanndraht, Schrauben, Kabelbinder, Pinholder und Heißkleber (Oasis), Trockenblumensteckschaum-Zylinder (Oasis)

artificial summer florals (Gasper), barley, dried grasses, cut tree trunks, burlap, wire mesh, tension wire screws, cable ties, pinholder and hot glue (Oasis), dry floral foam cylinder (Oasis)

Wie ein sichtbar gewordener sommerlicher Windhauch aus Feld und Flur wirkt dieser Tresen- oder Raumschmuck mit seiner gewellten Form.

With its wavy shape, this counter or room decoration conjures up the image of a breeze from a summer meadow.

Tips & Steps

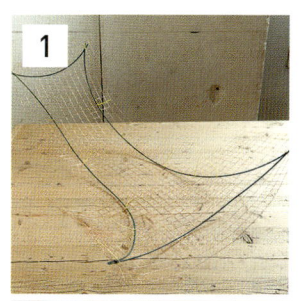

(1) Aus vier Spanndrahtstücken und Drahtgitter mithilfe von Kabelbindern eine längliche Form bilden. (2) Kaffeesack zurechtschneiden und auf den Draht kleben. (3) Diese Grundform auf die beiden Holzstämme legen und zusammen mit Pinholdern festschrauben. (4) Trockenblumensteckschaum-Zylinder aufstecken und zusätzlich mit Heißkleber fixieren. (5) Blüten und Gräser der Form entsprechend einstecken.

(1) Mould wire mesh and four tension wires into a longish shape and secure with cable ties. (2) Cut a burlap bag to size and glue to the wire. (3) Arrange this wavy shape over both tree trunks and hold in place with pinholders and screws. (4) Place a dry floral foam cylinder on each pinholder and additionally hot-glue. (5) Insert flowers and grasses in keeping with the shape.

Cool & Pure

Botanische Spezialisten

Aus hochwertigem Kunststoff sind Kakteen, Sukkulenten und zähblättrige Bromelien optisch überzeugend nachzubilden. Aus diesen Kunstpflanzen geschaffene Naturszenen oder Floralskulpturen begeistern mit Wüsten-Look, Urwald-Flair oder der Faszination einer botanischen Sammlung.

Botanical specialists

Convincing-looking replicas of cacti, succulents and bromeliads with fleshy leaves can be made with high-quality plastic. Nature landscapes and floral sculptures created with these artificial plants are a delight, be it in a desert look, with jungle flair or as fascinating botanical collection.

Zu diesem Thema gehören verschiedene Steine und verwitterte Hölzer sowie Sand als Elemente des natürlichen Umfelds.

This theme uses a variety of stones, weathered wood and sand as elements of natural environments.

Tillandsien sind als epiphytische Spezialisten an sich schon relativ anspruchslos. Für Raumsituationen, in denen sogar das notwendige Licht fehlt, bieten sich naturnah gestaltete Szenarien mit ihren Nachbildungen an.

Tillandsia is an expert epiphyte and therefore relatively undemanding. In room situations where not even the necessary light is present, lifelike scenarios can be designed with replicas.

künstliche Tillandsien (Gasper), Seetang, Äste, Moos, Steine, Wollkordel (Freese), Rebenbindedraht (Buco), Wickeldraht und Myrtendraht (Buco)

artificial Tillandsia (Gasper), seaweed, branches, moss, stones, wool string (Freese), florist's twine (Buco), winding wire and myrtle wire (Buco)

126 / 127

...tliche Tillandsien und Mooskrautstücke (Gasper), Treibholzstücke, Blasenflechte, Holzgefäße (Gasper), ...e, Sand, Steckdraht (Buco), Trockenblumensteckschaum-Ziegel (Oasis)

artificial Tillandsia and pieces of spike moss (Gasper), pieces of driftwood, *Hypogymnia*, wooden containers (Gasper), stones, sand, fixing wire (Buco), floral foam bricks (Oasis)

Wie ein Ausschnitt aus einem lange Zeit sich selbst überlassenen Pflasterweg erscheint diese Gestaltung mit Rosettenpflanzen.

This creation with rosette succulents looks like a cross-section of a cobblestone path that has not been tended for a long time.

künstliche Sukkulenten (Gasper), Moos, Steine, Zierdraht (Buco), Band (Goldina), Blechtisch (House Doctor)

artificial succulents (Gasper), moss, stones, deco wire (Buco), ribbon (Goldina), metal table (House Doctor)

128 / 129

An Stellen, an denen Wasser durch Gießen oder Übersprühen und ausreichendes Licht nicht zur Verfügung gestellt werden können, ermöglichen täuschend echte Pflanzennachbildungen den Anblick einer kleinen botanischen Sammlung.

In situations where water cannot be provided with an atomizer or watering can and the light is insufficient, remarkably realistic plant replicas can be made into a small botanical collection.

…liche Pflanzen in Töpfen (Gasper), Weinstöcke, … Band (Goldina), Blechschale

artificial plants in pots (Gasper), grapevines, sand, ribbon (Goldina), tin tray

Diese künstlichen Tillandsien ahmen die epiphytische Lebensweise ihrer natürlichen Vorbilder nach.

These artificial Tillandsia plants mimic the epiphytical growth habits of their natural role models.

Tips & Steps

(1) Zur Erzeugung nahezu echt aussehender Wurzeln Wollfäden in entsprechender Dicke zunächst in flüssiges Wachs tunken. (2) Unmittelbar danach die getränkte Wolle in Sand wälzen.

(1) To create almost lifelike roots, dip wool string of a suitable thickness in liquid wax. (2) Then immediately roll the soaked wool in sand.

links: künstliche Tillandsien (Gasper), Treibholzstücke (Freese), Rentierflechte, Zierdraht (Buco), Sand, Wachs, Steine, Heißkleber (Oasis)

left: artificial Tillandsia (Gasper), pieces of driftwood (Freese), reindeer lichen, deco wire (Buco), sand, wax, rocks, hot glue (Oasis)

rechts: künstliche Tillandsien (Gasper), Treibholzstücke, Wolle (Freese), Sand, Wachs

right: artificial Tillandsia (Gasper), pieces of dri wood, wool (Freese), sand, wax

130 / 131

Für die natürliche Anmutung dieser künstlichen Pflanzungen sind sowohl die tragenden Steine oder Holzknorren wichtig, als auch die Pflanzenkombination und das naturähnliche Zurechtbiegen der Triebe.

For achieving the natural look of these artificial plantings, the rocks and gnarled roots in the base are just as important as the combination of plants and the lifelike way the shoots are bent.

künstliche Sukkulenten (Gasper), Rentierflechte, Wolle (Freese), Sand, Wachs, Wickeldraht (Buco), Heißkleber (Oasis)

above: artificial succulents (Gasper), reindeer lichen, wool (Freese), sand, wax, winding wire (Buco), hot glue (Oasis)

unten: künstliche Sukkulenten (Gasper), Holzrinde, Blasenflechte, Wolle (Freese), Wachs, Heißkleber und Trockenblumensteckschaum-Ziegel (Oasis)

below: artificial succulents (Gasper), tree bark, *Hypogymnia*, wool (Freese), wax, hot glue, dry floral foam bricks (Oasis)

oben: künstliche Sukkulenten im Betongefäß (Gasper), *Leucophyta brownii*, Steine, Rebenbindedraht (Buco), Trockenblumensteckschaum-Ziegel (Oasis)

above: artificial succulents in concrete pot (Gasper), *Leucophyta brownii*, stones, florist's twine (Buco), dry floral foam bricks (Oasis)

> Gestalterische Prinzipien bei Pflanzungen, hier unregelmäßige Reihung, Gruppierung und asymmetrische Akzentuierung, finden auch bei der Verarbeitung dauerhafter Pflanzennachbildungen ihre Anwendung.
>
> Design principles for plantings, in this case irregular rows, groupings and asymmetrical highlighting, can also be applied when working with permanent plant replicas.

unten links: künstliche Fetthenne im Betongefäß (Gasper), Holzrinde (Freese), Steingranulatmatte, Wickeldraht (Buco)

bottom left: artificial Sedum in cement pot (Gasper), tree bark (Freese), granulated stone mat, winding wire (Buco)

unten rechts: künstliche Sukkulenten im Wurzelknorren (Gasper)

bottom right: artificial succulents in gnarled root (Gasper)

Die harmonische Ausstrahlung dieser künstlichen Pflanzung entsteht wesentlich durch die Formverwandtschaft zwischen den kreisrunden Sukkulenten-Rosetten und der annähernden Kugelform der gesamten Gestaltung.

The harmony radiated by these artificial plantings is created mostly by the similar shape of the round rosette succulents and the nearly round shape of the overall arrangement.

nstliche Sukkulenten-Rosetten (Gasper), Moos, Wurzelknorrengefäße (Freese), Trockenblumensteck- aum-Ziegel (Oasis), weitere im Bild sichtbare Elemente: Tisch (Broste)

artificial succulent roses (Gasper), moos, gnarled root containers (Freese), dry floral foam bricks (Oasis), other elements visible in the picture: table (Broste)

Tips & Steps

(1) Gebleichte Holzstückchen mit Heißkleber um den Topf der künstlichen Sukkulente kleben. (2) Den Topf in angerührte Gipsmasse tunken. (3) Der obere Teil der Holzstücke bleibt von Gips unbedeckt.

(1) Hot-glue bleached bits of wood around the pot of artificial succulents. (2) Dip the pot into a bowl of wet plaster. (3) Keep the upper part of the wood pieces free of plaster.

künstliche Kakteen und Euphorbien (Gasper), gebleichte Zweige, gebleichte Holzstücke, Keramikteller (D&M), Gips, Zierdraht (Buco), Steine

artificial cacti and Euphorbia (Gasper), bleached twigs, bleached pieces of wood, ceramic plate (D&M), plaster, deco wire (Buco), stones

134 / 135

Diese Sammlungen mit künstlichen Sukkulenten gefüllter Töpfe ermöglichen viele Variationen durch immer wieder neue Positionierungen und Kombinationen der Einzelbestandteile.

These collections of pots filled with artificial succulents offer many variations, simply by repositioning and combining the individual pieces.

künstliche Sukkulenten (Gasper), Holzrinde (Freese), nd (Goldina), Tablett (Dijk)

artificial succulents (Gasper), tree bark (Freese), ribbon (Goldina), tray (Dijk)

künstliche Sukkulenten und Tillandsien (Gasper), Blechgefäß (House Doctor), Töpfe, Steine, Granulat, Zement, Holzlatten und -bretter für die Schalung

artificial succulents and Tillandsia (Gasper), tin tray (House Doctor), pots, stones, granulate, cement, wooden slats and boards for the formwork

Künstliche Pflanzen ermöglichen eine Verarbeitung durch Eingießen in Beton, ohne dabei ihre naturhafte Ausstrahlung zu verlieren. Die zusätzliche Einarbeitung von Steinen unterstützt diesen Effekt.

Artificial plants can be embedded in concrete without losing their natural appearance. Adding stones will further enhance this effect.

Tips & Steps

136 / 137

(1) Aus ungehobelten Holzbrettern und -latten Schalkästen in gewünschter Größe zimmern. **(2)** Zement anrühren und in die Kästen gießen. **(3)** Die Sukkulenten und teils auch Steine einsetzen. Nach dem Trocknen und Erhärten des Zements die Holzschalung entfernen.

(1) Construct boxes of coarse wooden boards and slats in the desired sizes. **(2)** Mix cement and pour into the framework. **(3)** Arrange the succulents and some stones. After the cement has dried and hardened, remove the wooden moulds.

Ob als Gruppe aus Einzelpflanzen in Töpfen oder in einer Schale versammelt, diese Nachbildungen imposanter Sukkulenten vermitteln selbst in einem großen Raum die Exotik einer Halbwüste.

Whether as a group of individual plants in pots or assembled in a bowl, these replicas of imposing succulents convey the exotic look of a semi-arid savanna, even in a large room.

künstliche Agave, Säulen- und Feigenkakteen sowie Sansevierien (Gasper), Gefäße (Gasper), Kordeln (Freese), Stacheldraht, Steine, Trockenblumensteckschaum-Ziegel (Oasis)

artificial agave, columnar cactus, Opuntia, Sansevieria (all Gasper), containers (Gasper), string (Freese), barbed wire, stones, dry floral foam bricks (Oasis)

138 / 139

...stliche Kugelkakteen, Agaven, Säuleneuphorbien und Greiskraut-Arten (alle Gasper), Gefäße (Gasper), ...e, Trockenblumensteckschaum-Ziegel (Oasis)

artificial barrel cactus, agaves, columnar Euphorbia and Senecio (all Gasper), containers (Gasper), stones, dry floral foam bricks (Oasis)

Während das Opuntien-Duo seinen festen Stand durch gegossene Betonwürfel mit Metallstab erhält, wird das Säuleneuphorbien-Trio durch zylinderförmige Betonbohrkerne stabilisiert.

While the Opuntia duet gets a firm foothold from metal rods in poured concrete cubes, the trio of columnar Euphorbia is stabilized by cylindrical concrete drill cores.

künstliche Opuntien (Gasper), Weinrebenstücke (Gasper), Betonfuß (Freese), Zierdraht (Buco), Rebenbindedraht und Heißkleber (Oasis)

artificial Opuntia (Gasper), pieces of winestock (Gasper), concrete foot (Freese), deco wire (Buco), florist's twine, hot glue (Oasis)

Tips & Steps

1

2

3

(1) Fahrradschlauch aufschneiden und in Stücke zerteilen, deren Länge dem Umfang der Bohrkerne entspricht. (2) An den Enden der Stücke Nietösen anbringen. (3) Gebleichte Wurzelstöcke an den Bohrkern legen und mit den Schlauchstücken sowie eingefädelter Kordel festbinden.

(1) Cut open the bicycle hose and cut into pieces the length of the drill cores. (2) Attach eyelets to the ends to thread in strings. (3) Attach bleached rootstocks to the side of the drill core and hold in place with the pieces of hose and strings.

140 / 141

stliche Säuleneuphorbien (Gasper), gebleichte zelstöcke, Nietösen, Fahrradreifenschlauch, del, Betonbohrkerne

artificial columnar Euphorbia (Gasper), bleached rootstocks, eyelets, bicycle tire tube, string, concrete drill core

Natürlich!
Der Spezialist für Naturprodukte in der Floristik

Eigene Produktkreationen und ein umfangreiches Sortiment mit aktuellen Saison-Neuheiten machen uns zu einem kompetenten Partner des floristischen Großhandels. Unsere Stärke ist die Spezialisierung auf naturverbundene Dekorationen kunsthandwerklich verarbeiteten Pflanzenmaterialien.

Natural!
Spezialized in natural products for florists

Our own product creations and a comprehensive range of products, including up-to-the-minute seasonal novelties, makes us a competent partner for florist wholesalers. Our strength ist he specialization in natural decorations with handcrafted natural materials.

HF nature trends

HEINR · FREESE GmbH
IMPORT-EXPORT
Lütjenburger Straße 107
D–23714 Bad Malente
T +49 (0)4523 9894-0
F +49 (0)4523 9894-19
info@heinr-freese.de
www.heinr-freese.de

Am Puls der Zeit mit künstlichen Blumen und Pflanzen

Als Vollsortimenter im Bereich künstlicher Blumen und Pflanzen, als Spezialist für Kunst-Bäume bis zu einer Höhe von vier Metern und Lieferant von Dekorations- und Geschenkartikeln für Haus und Garten gehört Gasper zu den führenden Unternehmen der Branche.

Contemporary with artificial flowers and plants

As stockist of a wide range of artificial flowers and plants, specialising in artificial trees up to four metres high, gifts and decorative accessories for home and garden, Gasper is one of the industry's leading suppliers.

GASPER GmbH
ACCESSOIRES FÜR HAUS UND GARTEN
Am Grott 4
D–51147 Köln
T +49 (0)2203 96669-0
F +49 (0)2203 96669-41
gasper@gasper.de
www.gasper.de

Impressum / Imprint

HERAUSGEBER / PUBLISHER
BLOOM's GmbH, Ratingen (D)

KONZEPTION / CONCEPT
Klaus Wagener, Radko Ivanov Chapov

FLORISTIK / FLORISTRY
Radko Ivanov Chapov, Anja Hellner, Doreen Neumann, Michael Sutmöller, Bernhild Wagener, Klaus Wagener

CHEFREDAKTION / EDITOR IN CHIEF
Hella Henckel

TEXT / TEXT
Karl-Michael Haake

GRAFIK DESIGN / GRAPHIC DESIGN
Adriani Schmidt

DTP / DTP
Britta Baschen

FOTOS / PHOTOGRAPHY
Patrick Pantze Images GmbH, Lage (D)

ÜBERSETZUNG / TRANSLATION
Jessica Brümmer, Düsseldorf (D)

DRUCK / PRINT
Firmengruppe APPL, aprinta Druck, Wemding (D)

© BLOOM's GmbH
Am Potekamp 6 | D-40885 Ratingen
T +49 2102 9644-0 | F +49 2102 896073
info@blooms.de | www.blooms.de
1. Auflage 2017 / 1st Edition 2017
ISBN 978-3-945429-64-8

Das Werk ist urheberrechtlich geschützt. Jede Verwertung ist ohne schriftliche Zustimmung des Verlags oder des Herausgebers unzulässig. Dies gilt insbesondere für Vervielfältigungen, Übersetzungen, Mikroverfilmungen sowie deren Einspeicherung und Verarbeitung in elektronischen Systemen.

This material is protected by copyright law. Any utilization without the written permission of the publisher or editor is prohibited and liable to prosecution. This also applies to reproductions, translations and microfilm records as well as storage and processing in electronic systems.

Dank / Thanks

Wir danken folgenden Firmen für die Zurverfügungstellung ihrer Produkte:

We would like to thank the following companies for supplying their products:

Gasper – www.gasper.de
Heinr. Freese – www.heinr-freese.de

sowie / furthermore

Affari – www.affari.nu
Bloomingville – www.bloomingville.com
Broste – www.brostecopenhagen.com
BUCO – www.buco-wire.com
Chilewich – www.chilewich.com
D&M Depot – www.dmdepot.be
Dutz – www.dutz.nl
Fink – www.fink-living.de
Goldina – www.goldina.de
House Doctor – www.housedoctor.dk
Lehner – www.lehnerwolle3.com
Leonardo – www.leonardo.de
Serax – www.serax.com
Smithers-Oasis – www.oasisfloral.de
Zwiesel – www.zwiesel-kristallglas.com

Das in diesem Buch vielfach erwähnte **Drillgerät** (Twister) von Buco ist im gut sortierten Fachhandel und unter **www.blooms.de/diy-zubehoer** erhältlich.

The Buco **hand drill** (twister) often mentioned in this book is available at well-stocked specialist retailers and at **www.blooms.de/diy-zubehoer.**

Wir danken für die Überlassung von Räumen und Freigelände zum Fotografieren:

We would like to thank the following companies for granting us the use of their rooms or premises for staging and photographing:

Facharztezentrum, Minden
Golfclub Am Harrl e. V., Bad Eilsen
Restaurant Elliniko, Bad Oeynhausen
Wilhelm Altendorf GmbH & Co. KG, Minden
Staatsbad Bad Oeynhausen
Kirchengemeinde St. Walburga, Porta Westfalica

Wir danken allen Fotografen, Models, Kreativen und Mitarbeitern von der Logistik bis zur Verwaltung, die mit ihrem Engagement zum Gelingen dieses Buches beigetragen haben.

We would like to thank all the photographers, models, creatives and employees, from logistics to administration, for their commitment, which has contributed to the success of this book.